Studies in Jeremiah

Studies in

JEREMIAH

Clyde T. Francisco

Convention Press

NASHVILLE   **TENNESSEE**

Code Number: Church Study Course
This book is number 0227 in category 2, section
for Adults and Young People

Library of Congress Catalog Card Number: 61–12661
Printed in the United States of America
380. JY 61 R.R.D.

TO NANCY LEE, MY WIFE

My "Inn in the Wilderness"

Jeremiah 9:2

About the Author

CLYDE T. FRANCISCO was born in Virgilina, Virginia, June 2, 1916. When he was very young, his family moved to Danville, Virginia, where he received his public school training. His college education was pursued at the University of Richmond, where he achieved the highest average ever made at that institution and also played varsity football.

His pastorates include Woodlawn Baptist Church, Danville, Virginia; Gwathmey Baptist Church, Ashland, Virginia; Turner Ridge Baptist Church, Falmouth, Kentucky; and Bedford Baptist Church, Bedford, Kentucky. In 1942 he received his Th.M. degree from The Southern Baptist Theological Seminary, and in 1944 his Th.D. Upon his graduation he remained at Southern Seminary as an instructor in Old Testament. He is now John R. Sampey Professor of Old Testament Interpretation at that institution.

He has written for *The Adult Teacher,* prepared Training Union program materials for Young People, and is the author of *Introducing the Old Testament.* As one of the translators, he contributed to *The Berkeley Version of the Holy Bible.* He is one of the revisers of the *International Standard Bible Encyclopedia.*

Dr. and Mrs. Francisco have two children, a son Don, and a daughter Carol Lee.

Contents

Church Study Course

THE CHURCH STUDY COURSE began October 1, 1959. It is a merger of three courses previously promoted by the Sunday School Board—the Sunday School Training Course, the Graded Training Union Study Course, and the Church Music Training Course. On October 1, 1961, the Woman's Missionary Union principles and methods studies were added.

The course is fully graded. The system of awards provides a series of five diplomas of twenty books each for Adults or Young People, two diplomas of five books each for Intermediates, and two diplomas of five books each for Juniors. Book awards earned previously in the Sunday School Training Course, the Graded Training Union Study Course, and the Church Music Training Course may be transferred to the new course.

The course is comprehensive with books grouped into twenty categories. The purpose of the course is to help Christians to grow in knowledge and conviction, to help them to grow toward maturity in Christian character and competence for service, to encourage them to participate worthily as workers in their churches, and to develop leaders for all phases of church life and work.

The Church Study Course is promoted by the Baptist Sunday School Board, 127 Ninth Avenue, North, Nashville, Tennessee, through its Sunday School, Training Union, Church Music, and Church Administration departments; and the Woman's Missionary Union, 600 North Twentieth Street, Birmingham, Alabama; and by the respective departments in the states affiliated with the Southern Baptist Convention. A complete description of the course and the system of awards may be found in the catalog *Church Study Course,* which may be obtained without charge from any one of these departments.

A record of all awards earned should be maintained in each church. A person should be designated by the church to keep the files. Forms for such records may be ordered from any Baptist Book Store.

Requirements for Credit in Class
or Home Study

IF CREDIT IS DESIRED for the study of this book in a class or by home study, the following requirements must be met:

I. IN CLASSWORK

1. The class must meet a minimum of seven and one-half clock hours. The required time does not include assembly periods. Ten class periods of forty-five minutes each are recommended. (If laboratory or clinical work is desired in specialized or technical courses, this requirement may be met by six clock hours of classwork and three clock hours of supervised laboratory or clinical work.)

2. A class member who attends all class sessions and completes the reading of the book within a week following the last class session will not be required to do any written work.

3. A class member who is absent from one or more class sessions must answer the questions on all chapters he misses. In such a case, he must turn in his paper within a week, and he must certify that he has read the book.

4. The teacher should request an award for himself. A person who teaches a book in the section for Intermediates or Juniors of any category or conducts an approved unit of instruction for Nursery, Beginner, or Primary children will be granted an award in category 11, Special Studies, which will count as an elective on his own diploma. He should specify in his request the name of the book taught, or the unit conducted for Nursery, Beginner, or Primary children.

5. The teacher should complete the "Request for Book Awards —Class Study" (Form 150) and forward it within two weeks after the completion of the class to the Church Study Course Awards Office, 127 Ninth Avenue, North, Nashville 3, Tennessee.

II. IN HOME STUDY

1. A person who does not attend any class session may receive credit by answering all questions for written work as indicated in the book. When a person turns in his paper on home study, he must certify that he has read the book.

2. Students may find profit in studying the text together, but individual papers are required. Carbon copies or duplicates in any form cannot be accepted.

3. Home study work papers may be graded by the pastor or a person designated by him, or they may be sent to the Church Study Course Awards Office for grading. The form entitled "Request for Book Awards—Home Study" (Form 151) must be used in requesting awards. It should be mailed to Church Study Course Awards Office, 127 Ninth Avenue, North, Nashville 3, Tennessee.

III. CREDIT FOR THIS BOOK

This book is number 0227 in category 2, section for Adults and Young People.

Introduction

A BOOK IS NEVER the work of one man, particularly if the author seeks to interpret the Bible. This volume is the result of many years of study under able men of God, and the interchange between students and teacher from which the instructor receives the greater benefit. Particular indebtedness must be acknowledged to Dr. James Leo Green, now professor of Old Testament Interpretation at Southeastern Baptist Theological Seminary, whose contributions are obvious to anyone familiar with his moving expositions of this great book of prophecy.

It has been impossible in the space available to produce a verse by verse commentary upon the book of Jeremiah. The student who is interested in this type of study should consult *The Expositor's Bible* or *Cambridge Bible*. What has been attempted here is an exposition of the principal truths to be found in Jeremiah's life and message. It is hoped that this type of work will both encourage further study and help the reader to grasp the relevance of the Old Testament for life today.

Any scriptural quotations not otherwise marked are from the King James Version, except when the author is giving his own translation or paraphrase. Special gratitude is expressed to Dr. C. Aubrey Hearn, the editor of the book, who patiently endured the delaying tactics of the author.

The last chapter of the book deals with Jeremiah 34–36. This does not mean that the author failed to finish his book. Chapters 37–52 are dealt with in summary fashion in the first chapter. It is not felt that all the meaning of these chapters, or of the book of Jeremiah, is exhausted in this exposition. We introduce the reader to Jeremiah and trust that many years of more intimate fellowship will follow.

CLYDE T. FRANCISCO
Louisville, Kentucky

CHAPTER 1 OUTLINE

I. THE HISTORICAL BACKGROUND
  1. The Reforms of Josiah
  2. The Tyranny of Egypt
  3. The Rule of Babylon
  4. The Fall of Jerusalem

II. THE PROPHET JEREMIAH
  1. Personal Characteristics
  2. Jeremiah the Poet
  3. The Life of Jeremiah

III. THE BOOK
  1. The Apparent Chaos of the Chronology
  2. The History of the Book

1

The Book and Its Author

No BOOK OF THE OLD TESTAMENT is more dependent upon a knowledge of its times for its interpretation than the book of Jeremiah. During Jeremiah's ministry the Jewish nation passed through many phases in a remarkably brief period. From the time he was called in 626 B.C. until the destruction of Jerusalem in 587, he saw his beloved people fall from the pinnacle of confident hope to the depths of despair. First Judah was subject to Assyria, then to Egypt and Babylon. Five kings reigned in Jerusalem during that span. One was killed in battle, another taken as prisoner to Egypt, and two exiled in Babylon. The best of the people were deported, and in the end the city was completely destroyed. Such a debacle needs careful consideration lest it happen again.

I. THE HISTORICAL BACKGROUND

A study of the discoveries of modern archaeology and the biblical records provides an accurate and comprehensive picture of what was happening in this momentous crisis in human history.

1. *The Reforms of Josiah*

The good king Hezekiah had been succeeded by one of Judah's worst, Manasseh. During his long reign the Hebrew nation drifted away from the high purpose of Isaiah, and foreign cults and practices were encouraged. Temple worship was de-emphasized, and the building itself was allowed to deteriorate. Manasseh was branded by the author of the books of Kings as possibly the worst king ever to sit on David's throne (cf. 2 Kings 21:9-15; 24:3 f.).

All this was reversed after Josiah came to the throne at the tender age of eight. Nothing is known of the years immediately following his coronation, but by 628 B.C. he was beginning to recover the territory lost to Assyria when Samaria fell a century before. Repairs upon the Temple were begun in preparation for the renewal of the ancient faith of Israel. In 622 an electrifying discovery was made. The book of the covenant was rediscovered in the Temple. This book was substantially the present book of Deuteronomy, which became the basis for the most sweeping reform in Israel's history. Both Judah and the territory of Northern Israel were purged of all alien practices and the public worship of Yahweh (Jehovah) was confined to the Jerusalem Temple. Plainly this reformation was political as well as religious. It amounted to a complete break with Assyria.

Such a maneuver was made possible by the fact that Assyria's empire was crumbling. Her kings were too busy securing the throne at home to be able to bother with the affairs of Palestine. Babylon and Media were applying increasing pressure upon Assyria. Surprisingly enough the latter found an unexpected ally in Egypt, which had been her deadly enemy for over a hundred years. It seems that Egypt had a remarkable facility for choosing the losing side.

In 612 B.C. Nineveh, the capital of Assyria, fell before Cyaxares, king of Media, and Nabopolassar, king of Babylon, although the Assyrian army continued the fight as it retreated west toward its allies in Egypt. In 609 Pharaoh Neco set out to join the Assyrians in a desperate attempt to push back the onrushing tide from the East. Perceiving the Egyptian purpose, Josiah, apparently hoping that he would fare better in face of a Babylonian victory, attempted to stop Neco. Instead, Josiah was killed and great consternation struck Judah. The mourning of the grieving nation became proverbial (cf. Zech. 12:11).

2. The Tyranny of Egypt

When Josiah was killed, his son Jehoahaz (Shallum) was made king in Jerusalem. Fearing further trouble from that direction, Neco, who was in Syria at the time, summoned Jehoahaz after only three months upon the throne, and deported him to Egypt. In his place Neco put Jehoahaz' brother Eliakim, whose name was changed to Jehoiakim, and made sure that he would remain an Egyptian vassal. Heavy tribute was placed upon Judah. She had only changed a distant master for one closer home.

Jehoiakim turned out to be a dismal failure. Concerned only for his own comfort and security, he cared little for the desperate plight of his subjects. The old pagan cults of the Manasseh era crept in again, amid the accompanying immorality. However, the impetus of the Josianic reforms kept the worship at the Temple in full swing, since it remained the center of Israel's nationalistic hopes. Yet this worship was merely form without the moral and ethical consciousness of the historic Mosaic faith. Large crowds brought many offerings, but the worshipers saw no necessity to examine their injustice to their neighbors, or their own lack of surrender to the redemptive purpose of Israel's God.

3. The Rule of Babylon

Events were hastening toward a climax. In 605 B.C. Nebuchadnezzar completely routed the Egyptians at Carchemish, and Jehoiakim was forced to shift his allegiance to Babylon. Yet there remained a strong pro-Egyptian group in Jerusalem, which was always insisting that Judah attempt to align itself with Egypt in an effort to throw off the Babylonian yoke. Jehoiakim himself favored this policy, which turned out to be ill advised. Nebuchadnezzar, after battling Pharaoh Neco to an apparent standstill in 601, retired to lick his wounds. This occasion encouraged Judah to rebel against him. Immediately Babylonia sent contingents to Palestine, and by 598 the main army arrived in Judah. Jehoiakim's mysterious death occurred at this time, and occasioned the crowning of his son Jehoiachin (Coniah). This unfortunate lad ruled only three months and was taken captive to Babylon in 597. Along with him were taken the leading citizens of Judah, numbering at least ten thousand, as well as priceless vessels from the Temple. Jehoiachin's uncle, Zedekiah (Mattaniah), was placed upon the throne by Nebuchadnezzar.

4. *The Fall of Jerusalem*

The folly of Jehoiakim left Judah in dire straits. Many of her cities lay in ruins, with her population depleted. From an estimated population in the eighth century of 250,000, the nation had now shrunk to half that size, the captivity of 597 B.C. culminating the process. Zedekiah did nothing but accelerate this downward rush. He appears to be the sort of monarch who had the best of intentions but lacked the courage of conviction (Jer. 37:17 to 38:28). Some of this was due to uncertainty about his authority. Apparently Jehoiachin was still regarded as the rightful king, although he was in exile (Ezek. 1:2). Many Jews expected his early return to reassume the throne (Jer. 27-29). In the face of this Zedekiah on the one hand was hesitant to arouse the opposition of his lords and on the other hand was anxious to prove his own prowess. Both inclinations pointed toward a rebellion against Babylon, which turned out to be the most futile move of all.

Once more Nebuchadnezzar made his way to Judah in January, 588, and was soon encamped before Jerusalem. News of the approach of Pharaoh Hophra led him to lift the siege momentarily, but he was soon back after quickly disposing of Egypt. When Jerusalem finally fell in July, 587, Nebuchadnezzar, infuriated by Judah's constant provocations, killed most of the people and took comparatively few prisoners. Among these, however, was Zedekiah, who was blinded and taken to Babylon in chains, where he died. Even as Northern Israel had perished in 722 B.C., just so the monarchy of Judah disintegrated in the blast of the wrath of God.

II. THE PROPHET JEREMIAH

In the trying times that marked the end of Judah as a nation, God called to speak for him a man who felt that of all men he was the most unlikely for the task, but who turned out to be the very one to declare what was in the mind of God.

1. Personal Characteristics

In Jeremiah it can be seen vividly that the greatest success is often found in apparent failure.

When he tried to arrest the course of a nation, only to be thrown down and trampled underfoot, when he cried out in bitterness of heart against the inexorable Will that compelled a poet to become a prophet, and a lover of men to be counted their enemy, he little knew that the development and record of his own lonely experience of failure was to be a success of the highest rank and influence.[1]

Although Jeremiah grieved constantly over the sins of Judah and cried out to God in his own trouble, the popular description, "weeping prophet," is hardly accurate in respect to him. The term is no more applicable than it would be to Jesus because he wept over Jerusalem. Jeremiah was no

---

[1] H. Wheeler Robinson, *The Cross in the Old Testament* (Philadelphia: Westminster Press, 1955), p. 121.

spineless weakling who idled away his days in wringing his hands over the sad plight of man.

> He called himself one born to be at odds with and in opposition to the whole world; and, while he lamented the necessity, he never flinched from the task. Wherever his figure emerges into distinctness, it is militant.[2]

Jeremiah's words were so stinging, so provocative that it was inevitable that those whom he criticized would attempt to destroy him. The situation was so serious, however, that he could only hope that by sacrificing himself he could save the nation. The ideal that some people have for a pastor, that he first of all be a "good mixer" or one who keeps everybody happy and content, is hardly applicable when impending destruction is hanging heavy over his people's heads. They must be warned whatever the cost to himself or to the harmony of the fellowship. People are prone to praise Jeremiah and criticize present-day prophets. When will men learn to heed their prophets rather than silence them?

Indeed, the time-honored words of Milton in *Paradise Lost* well describe the prophet Jeremiah:

> Servant of God, well done! well hast thou fought
> The better fight, who single hast maintained
> Against revolted multitudes the cause
> Of truth, in word mightier than they in arms.

2. *Jeremiah the Poet*

Much of the book of Jeremiah is in poetry. This is difficult for the English reader to grasp, for Hebrew poetry is not marked by rhyme, but by a regularity of rhythm. It resembles modern free verse and is likewise unhampered by artificial attempts to devise a rhyming scheme. The poet is free to express himself naturally.

---

[2] Adam C. Welch, *Jeremiah, His Time and His Work* (London: Oxford University Press, 1951), p. 1.

When the King James Version was made, Old Testament scholars lacked the knowledge necessary to distinguish Hebrew prose from poetry. More recent discoveries now make this possible in most places. It is necessary to turn to a modern translation, therefore, in order to recognize the literary character of Jeremiah's oracles. Many scholars have contended that he used poetry exclusively, and that the prose sections have been added by later editors, but such a claim is without proper proof. Although Jeremiah's lyric poetry characterizes his most stirring passages, yet not even a Jeremiah could always be poetically minded. Life becomes prosaic for everyone at times, even for an immortal prophet.

3. *The Life of Jeremiah*

Jeremiah was firmly rooted in the times in which he lived. Born in Anathoth of the priestly line of Abiathar, who had been removed from authority in Judah by Solomon (cf. 1 Kings 1:28 to 2:26), he was not likely to have escaped seeing every flaw in the Zadokite form of worship in Jerusalem. His home town was only three miles from the capital city, yet it was in northern Israelite territory, and decidedly rural in its way of life. The lad grew up loving the simple ways of life, in an atmosphere of culture and devotion.

In 626 B.C. he was called to preach. How old he was at the time is not known. The descriptive word he uses for himself ("a child") can be used of anyone from age one to age forty, but properly means a youth. A safe estimate would be that he was around twenty years old. Thus he would have been approximately sixty when Jerusalem fell in 587. His earlier preaching, found in chapters 1–6, seems to have culminated in a preaching tour urging the people to heed the word of God found in the rediscovered book of Deuteronomy (11:1 ff.). This book, which emphasized exclusive public worship at the Jerusalem Temple, must have been received with hostility in Anathoth, where the Abiathar priests continued to function independently of Jerusalem. This probably explains the attempt of the men of Anathoth to kill Jeremiah (11:18–23). They considered him a traitor to the family traditions. Their attack upon him was Jeremiah's first taste of persecution. He was reminded that this was only a prelude to the coming struggles (12:5).

Strangely, there are no prophecies from Jeremiah that can be placed with certainty in the period from the rediscovery of the law to the death of Josiah (622–609). No doubt he was preaching and some of his oracles were preserved, but they cannot be isolated. In fact, it must be admitted that he was at least in semiretirement. Evidently this was due to the nature of Josiah's reforms. The great king had been busy bringing about changes in the direction desired by the prophet. There was little for him to criticize in Josiah, in contrast to the kings that followed. In one place Jeremiah implied, however, that he had doubts about the sincerity of the people as they carried out Josiah's proclamations: "And yet for all this her treacherous sister Judah hath not turned unto me with her whole heart, but feignedly" (Jer. 3:10). Here Jeremiah admitted that there had been a turning to God, but more in outward form than inward consecration. The dubious nature of the reform in Judah was such that apparently Jeremiah took a cautious attitude toward the entire situation. He would wait and see, but what he saw now was not encouraging.

With the death of Josiah, however, Jeremiah returned to an active ministry. He saw nothing in Jehoiakim to admire and became quite certain that his policies would lead to the ruin of Judah. He began openly to attack the sins of the people. In his famous Temple Sermon (chap. 7) he ridiculed their superstitious trust in the Temple and predicted its destruction as well as captivity for the whole nation. Chapter 26 tells the story of the people's reaction to the sermon. Jeremiah narrowly escaped with his life. Perhaps Pashur's putting Jeremiah in the stocks followed soon after (chap. 20).

After this, the prophet was forbidden by Jehoiakim to preach in public. He was "shut up," he told Baruch, whom he had summoned to be his scribe. Apparently this does not mean that he was physically restrained but rather that he was forbidden access to the Temple area (36 : 1 ff.). Baruch was called in because Jeremiah wanted all his prophecies of the preceding years written down and read before all the people. Perhaps when they heard the warning of God, they would repent before it was too late. The reading of the prophecies caused great concern among the people and certain of the nobles. In an unforgettable scene, however, Jehoiakim burned the prophet's writings in an open fire. Promptly Jeremiah redictated the words to Baruch.

It was during this period that Jeremiah went through devastating personal agony. It seemed that he was one against a whole world. He was forbidden to marry (16 : 1 ff.). No one would heed his message, particularly the king. Hate was returned for his love (18 : 18 ff.). He was tempted to quit trying, but could not escape his responsibility (20 : 9).

When Zedekiah came to the throne, he had an ear for the prophet and secretly respected him (38 : 14 ff.) Yet Jeremiah fared worse during his reign than at any previous time. This was due to Zedekiah's inability to stand by his convictions. He felt powerless to keep his nobles from persecuting Jeremiah for what they believed to be treason. In the hour of crisis, when the country was trying to make its last stand, Jeremiah was openly advocating surrender to Nebuchadnezzar as the only possible hope. He was weakening the defenders' will to fight. When Jeremiah, certain that his word was rejected, attempted to leave the doomed city of Jerusalem, he was falsely accused of deserting to the Babylonians (37 : 11 ff.). This was a natural suspicion, since he had been advocating turning Jerusalem over to them. Beaten and disheartened, he was thrown into a dungeon to die. Only the intervention of Zedekiah saved him. Allowed to spend his confinement in the court of the guard, he was guaranteed bread as long as the supply lasted.

Jeremiah's enemies would have none of this. The sight of him still alive was a reminder of his counsel of surrender. They demanded of Zedekiah that he turn Jeremiah over to them. Reluctantly he acceded to their demand (38:5). When they came upon Jeremiah, he was lowered into a dungeon whose floor was filthy mire. Given no food or water, he was doomed. This time, however, an Ethiopian eunuch pleaded with Zedekiah for Jeremiah, and strengthened the king's own will. Tenderly the eunuch raised Jeremiah to safety and returned him to the court of the prison, where he remained until Jerusalem fell. God moves in mysterious ways to protect his own.

Nebuchadnezzar's general, Nebuzaradan, took Jeremiah along with other prisoners in chains as far as Ramah. When Jeremiah was recognized, the Chaldean offered him his choice of going to Babylon to enjoy the bounty of the king or remaining in Judah. Before Jeremiah could answer, the Chaldean saw at once that the prophet had no love for the Babylonians. He could read in Jeremiah's eyes that he was no traitor: "Go back also to Gedaliah the son of Ahikam the son of Shaphan, whom the king of Babylon hath made governor over the cities of Judah, and dwell with him among the people" (40:5).

It is apparent that Jeremiah was so grief-stricken over the tragic fulfilment of his prophecies that he was incapable of making a decision. Nebuzaradan made it for him, as he perceived Jeremiah's basic inclination. The great prophet had found no satisfaction in the verification of his predictions. There was nothing of the "I told you so" in his attitude. What he had dreaded had come upon them, and it was more dreadful than even he had imagined.

The quiet days with Gedaliah, who was of the family that

had befriended Jeremiah (26:24), were the most peaceful ones of his life. It was during this period that he dreamed of the future glory of the people of God (chaps. 30–31). All too soon, however, the peace was over. How long Gedaliah ruled, we do not know, but probably not more than a few months. Being an honest man, Gedaliah could not believe in the intricacies of court intrigue. He was slain by a trusted friend, Ishmael, who in turn was routed by Johanan. The little remnant of the Jews who gathered about him were in a strait. Should they remain in Judah and risk the ire of Babylon, who might misinterpret the whole affair and execute one and all over this new act of violence? Or should they flee to Egypt and leave the land without a responsible remnant of true believers?

In their perplexity they called upon Jeremiah, secretly hoping that he would confirm their inclination, which was to flee into Egypt. Word from God was long in coming; in fact, it was ten days before Jeremiah was sure: They should remain in Judah. God would protect them from Babylon (42:7 ff.). This was not what the people wanted to hear. They accused Jeremiah of getting his word from Baruch, not from the Lord. By force he was taken with them into Egypt, for although they did not heed him, they still valued his counsel. Perhaps like some moderns, they felt they had paid some penance already when they listened to his condemnation of their behavior.

When Jeremiah arrived in Egypt, with Baruch still by his side, we have our last glimpse of him, still boldly condemning the exiles for their worship of heathen gods and their faithlessness to the God of their fathers. Tradition says he died in Egypt, among the nations to whom he was called to preach, faithful to the end.

III. The Book

The times in which Jeremiah lived and the kind of man

whom God called to preach to the crisis, have been examined. Now we can gain some insight into the nature of the book in which is preserved what is known about the prophet. Only as a person knows something of the book can he interpret properly what it has to say about Jeremiah.

1. *The Apparent Chaos of the Chronology*

Although more is known about Jeremiah than any other prophet because of the faithfulness of the scribe Baruch, yet the book is almost a hopeless jumble of unrelated prophecies. For instance, chapters 21 and 24 are dated during the reign of Zedekiah, while chapter 25 is dated during the reign of Jehoiakim. Chapters 27 and 28 are also from Zedekiah's reign, while 35 and 36 belong to the reign of Jehoiakim. The Hebrew exiles in Babylonia are comforted in a passage (31:10 ff.) that appears long before the one where the prediction of the exile is made to Jehoiakim (chap. 36). These are but a few examples of the chronological confusion that has led one writer to say:

> As a lad I started to read the Scripture through according to the familiar schedule, three chapters each week-day and five on Sunday, by which we were assured that in a single year we could complete the reading of the Book. I got safely through Numbers and Leviticus, even Proverbs did not altogether quench my ardor, but I stuck in the middle of Jeremiah and never got out. I do not blame myself, for how can a boy read Jeremiah in its present form and understand it? [3]

What is the explanation of this strange state of affairs? Jeremiah was the only one of the prophets who had a personal secretary. One would therefore expect that of all the prophets his career would be the most carefully recorded. Yet the opposite seems true. Is this Baruch's contribution to the biblical record?

---

[3] Harry Emerson Fosdick, *The Modern Use of the Bible* (New York: The Macmillan Company, 1924), p. 21.

Such questions as this led to a special study in this area.[4] The findings are recorded in a helpful expository study.[5] It is Dr. Wood's view, with which the author concurs, that materials found in the book of Jeremiah must have circulated in the form of separate scrolls, each of which contained his teachings upon certain subjects. The arrangement, therefore, is not chronological, but topical. These various scrolls have been combined to form the present book. Between the various scrolls have been inserted a number of stories from the life of Jeremiah. Proceeding upon this premise, seven major collections are found in the book.

I. The Earlier Prophecies of Jeremiah (chaps. 1–6, delivered primarily before 622 B.C.)
II. False and True Wisdom (8 : 4 to 10 : 25)
III. Pessimistic Messages (chaps. 11–20)
IV. Polemics Against Kings and Prophets (chaps. 22–29)
V. Passages of Hope (chaps. 30–33)
VI. Historical Section (chronologically arranged from the siege of Jerusalem through the flight into Egypt, chaps. 37–44)
VII. Foreign Prophecies (chaps. 46–51)

Between the first and second scrolls, Jeremiah's famous Temple Sermon has been inserted (chap. 7), and between rolls three and four a story of Jeremiah's advice during the siege of Jerusalem appears (chap. 21). Connecting collections five and six are three narratives dealing with Israel's reception of the word of God (chaps. 34–36). The story of Jeremiah's personal counsel to Baruch joins the historical section to the foreign prophecies (chap. 45), and a historical appendix is added as the last chapter (chap. 52). Seen in this light, the book of Jeremiah is definitely carefully put

---

[4] Fred M. Wood, "A Chronological Reconstruction of the Life and Prophecies of Jeremiah." Unpublished doctoral thesis, Southern Baptist Theological Seminary, 1948.

[5] Fred M. Wood, *Fire in My Bones* (Nashville: Broadman Press, 1959).

together. It is the attempt to arrange it chronologically that produces confusion.

2. The History of the Book

From chapter 36 it must be concluded that the messages of Jeremiah remained in oral form from 626 until 605 B.C. It is remarkable that Jeremiah could reproduce from memory what he had said during this period. Likely, as he recorded he also reinterpreted some of his older sayings. When this copy was burned by Jehoiakim, it was a simple matter to record the words again, but to them were added "many like words" (36:32). Chapters 1–25 are the result of this second recording, although they have been editorially rearranged. Within them have been inserted the "Confessions of Jeremiah," passages which reveal the inner life of the prophet, preserved by his faithful biographer, Baruch. The other sections of the book were added later as the result of the Jerusalem scribe's constant attendance upon the prophet. After Jeremiah died, the book went through its final editing, as did most of the Old Testament books.

Evidence of the difficulties of translation of the text is to be found in a comparison of the Greek and Hebrew manuscripts. The Greek Septuagint (translated between 250–100 B.C.) differs considerably from the traditional Hebrew Massoretic text. In fact, one eighth of the Hebrew text does not appear in the Septuagint. Even where the same passages occur, the sense is often different. These differences are variously explained: The Greek does not attempt to translate the received Hebrew text literally; the manuscripts were often illegible; many errors were unconscious mistakes of the copyists; some changes were intentional.

These explanations account for many of the divergent readings, but not the two most glaring discrepancies in the versions: the absence of so many passages in the Septuagint that appear in the Hebrew and the rearrangement of the foreign prophecy section.

The prophecies of Jeremiah against foreign nations appear in chapters 46–51. An analysis of their nature will be given at this point, since there will not be further opportunity to deal with them in this brief study. In this section are prophecies against Egypt (chap. 46), Philistia (chap. 47), Moab (chap. 48), Ammon (49:1–6), Edom (49:7–22), Syria (49:23–27), Arabia (49:28–33), Elam (49:34–39), and Babylon (chaps. 50–51). Similar sections are found in the books of Isaiah and Ezekiel.

Considerable light may have been thrown upon these mysterious and often unedifying passages of the prophets by recent discoveries in Egypt. The Execration Texts "illustrate how the Pharaoh sought to bring magical powers to bear on his enemies, actual or potential. In the first series, imprecations against various foes were inscribed on jars and bowls, which were then smashed—thus making the imprecation effective." [6] Although the Hebrew prophets did not employ the art of black magic, it is likely that there was some regular place in their sacred festival where a prophet would pronounce the wrath of Yahweh upon the enemies of Israel. This may have been accompanied by some symbolic act. Jeremiah's breaking of the vessel, which represented Judah (chap. 19), strongly resembles the practice revealed in the Execration Texts. Indeed, the inaugural sermon of Amos (Amos 1–2) takes on more meaning if he was expected to deliver such tirades against the heathen for the occasion, and then suddenly broke the pattern as he included Israel among the objects of divine wrath.

Such oracles of wrath upon Israel's enemies may bring little edification to a modern reader, since he has not felt the brunt

---

[6] John Bright, *A History of Israel* (Philadelphia: Westminster Press. Copyright 1959 by W. L. Jenkins), pp. 47–48.

of the hostilities of such foes. Yet they formed a continuing part of the Hebrew view of history. Their God would triumph over all the enemies of his people. The Christian of today finds his comfort as he reads these ancient polemics in the reassurance that the present enemies of the true faith will meet a like fate. It is popular today to preach concerning the divine wrath upon the sins of America, but it should not be forgotten that nations that openly defy God are due an even worse fate.

The foreign prophecies of Jeremiah, which appear in the English texts as chapters 46–51, in the Septuagint are found after verse 13 of chapter 25. How could this have happened? The only sensible explanation is that the translators of the Septuagint were using a Hebrew text that was different from the Massoretic that is used today. Apparently both the present Hebrew and the Greek have been derived from still earlier manuscripts, rather than the Septuagint having followed the Massoretic text. Which is more faithful to the original? Comparative studies of the two basic versions outside of the book of Jeremiah, as well as the evidence of the Dead Sea Scrolls, would favor the Massoretic text upon which our English translations are based. Yet the Greek may preserve some valuable older readings in an occasional passage.

When one realizes the many hands through which the book of Jeremiah has passed in its compilation and transmission, he marvels at the remarkable fidelity of its record. It could be only through the guidance of our Lord that the books of the Old Testament were preserved over long centuries of editing and copying. In the book of Jeremiah not only the faith of the prophet himself is found, but also that of the devout community of saints who compiled and preserved it. Thus in every book of the Old Testament God has chosen to speak both through an individual and the continuing community to which he belonged, which in the infinite grace of God now includes ourselves. As the teachings of the book are applied today, the reader becomes a part of the prophet's lengthened shadow.

FOR STUDY AND DISCUSSION

1. What is a prophet? Are prophets needed today? What would they say about us?
2. How do the conditions of Jeremiah's day parallel our own? List some similarities and differences.
3. Compare and contrast the character of Jeremiah and that of Jesus.
4. Rearrange the chapters in the book of Jeremiah in chronological order.

CHAPTER 2 OUTLINE

I. THE CALL (1:1–19)
   1. Contrast with Isaiah and Ezekiel
   2. Personal Predestination to Service
   3. The Prophet's Reluctance
   4. The Enabling Power of God
   5. The Nature of the Ministry
   6. The Reaffirmation of the Call

II. THE EARLY MINISTRY (2:1 to 6:30)
   1. Contrast of Israel's Present with Her Past (2:1–13)
   2. The Nature of Sin (2:14–37)
   3. The Consequences of Sin (2:14–37)
   4. Hope for the Hopeless (3:1 to 4:4)
   5. Oracles of Doom (4:5 to 6:30)

2

Jeremiah's Call and Early Ministry

Jeremiah 1:1 to 6:30

THE CALL OF JEREMIAH foreshadowed the character of his ministry. A clear understanding of the essential elements in the call gives the key to an understanding of his preaching of later years. The God-called man today goes through the same experience. He never can get away from the impressions that first led him to surrender to God. They will underlie everything he says and does in the years that follow.

I. THE CALL (1:1-19)

The call of Jeremiah is placed in its proper historical setting in the opening verses of the book. He was from the priestly line of Anathoth and began his ministry in the thirteenth year of Josiah (626 B.C.).

1. Contrast with Isaiah and Ezekiel

The inauguration of Jeremiah's prophetic career is presented in stark contrast to that of Isaiah and Ezekiel. Both their calls (Isa. 6; Ezek. 1) were accompanied by glorious visions of God and his heavenly attendants. Overcome by a sense of national and personal sin, Isaiah cried out in dismay before the holy God who appeared before him. Likewise Ezekiel fell down upon his face before the glorious spectacle of the reigning God. When Jeremiah was called, however, there were no heavenly visions, but simply "the word of the Lord came unto me saying" (1:4). God spoke to him as a familiar friend, one who was already in intimate fellowship with him. In Jeremiah's reaction there was no sense of sin or

19

overwhelming glory of God. He appears to have taken the encounter naturally, as if the two of them had met before, and had already become fast friends. His surprise came not from the encounter but from the nature of the demands of God. It is clear, therefore, that the call of Jeremiah was the natural fruition of a relationship with God that had begun long before and had already deepened into an abiding fellowship. In this meeting Jeremiah was given insight for the first time into what the nature of his divine mission was to be. At this point the boy became a man.

2. Personal Predestination to Service

Jeremiah came to realize that before he was born God had purposed that he should be a prophet to the nations. The time had come for prophecy to come out of the shell of nationalism and speak to the world. No prophet could speak for God in the times in which Jeremiah lived unless he addressed the world. It was no age for narrowness or provincialism, and in this respect it parallels our own time. Our day also is an age of world-shaking events. A modern prophet of God cannot preach a message that is addressed only to his own region of the country or to his own select group. The times call for a divine message to the world, directing men to find their place under God in this confused generation. Although Jeremiah did not preach directly to the Babylonians or Egyptians, he was kept busy instructing his own people concerning how to live in a world that included them. Such is the task of today's preacher and teacher. Men can no longer be exclusively concerned about their own country. Every other nation is suddenly in one's own back yard.

Jeremiah was predestined to have an international ministry before he came into the world. Here is a classic example of election to service. One must look elsewhere for the doctrine of election to salvation. When God said he "knew" him and "ordained" him before birth, he did not mean that Jeremiah had no choice in the matter. Jeremiah could have refused the appointment; but if he had done so, he would have missed his destiny. Any other path would have meant nothing but uselessness and hopelessness. God plans a man's life but the man may say no at his own peril. God's work will go on, but the man will be cast aside as the tide of history moves on.

Whom God predestines, he prepares. Before Jeremiah was aware of his destiny, God was getting him ready for his moment in history. How did God prepare him?

(1) *His place of birth and boyhood.*—The priests of Anathoth were rebels from the first, and their spirit was in Jeremiah. Also the rural background in Anathoth gave him many of his striking figures of speech. Being three miles from Jerusalem, he was able to attend all the festival occasions there. He was close enough to Jerusalem to know it, and far enough away to be objective about it. This position can produce an ideal critic.

(2) *His family.*—"Jeremiah" means "Yahweh (the Lord) hurls." This descriptive name, given to the newborn infant during the dark days of Manasseh's reign, pictures the hope of his parents that God would use their son in the furious battle against God's enemies. Although his mother's name is not known, she must have been a major influence upon her son. His sensitive spirit reveals a man who was well taught by a discerning woman. Women are the principal civilizing force in society. If a man's mother fails to get him out of the jungle, a good wife soon will. A remarkable change for the better came over the atmosphere of the dining hall of a seminary when women were allowed to have their meals there also. Both the father and the mother of Jeremiah trained their son well. A youth does not learn to walk with God at such an early age unless someone has given him a good beginning.

(3) *The earlier prophets.*—Jeremiah was profoundly influenced by the prophets who had preached before him, par-

ticularly Hosea, who was also a northern Israelite. Jeremiah held the essential ideas of Hosea: religion is a fellowship with God; sin breaks the heart of God; the wrath of God is an awful force; God's mercy to the penitent is tender. In one significant way he did not follow the earlier prophet: he took no chance on marriage! Perhaps Hosea's unhappy experience, as well as the unsettled times (Jer. 16), discouraged him.

All people are more dependent upon those who have gone before them than they realize. We do well to preserve what is good in our past, and build upon that. It is foolish to start from scratch in every generation. We do not live long enough to catch up. Yet we must not be slaves to the past. Jeremiah depended heavily upon Hosea in his early ministry (chaps. 1–6), but soon began to develop his own style of preaching that could never be confused with the earlier prophet. We do well to start where others have left off, but eventually we must learn to be ourselves.

Thus God prepared Jeremiah for his task, as he is preparing the reader. What does he want of you in the future? Often the clue can be found in your past. Whatever God has yet for you to do, he has been preparing you for it. What did you dream when you were a child, before this materialistic age drowned out your vision? That dream could have been placed there by God. Now that you have become an adult, your childish dreams may need to be applied to a more mature purpose; yet from them some direction may come. It is certain that the God who leads you into tomorrow was at work in your life yesterday preparing you for today and the years ahead. One may often discover the future in the past.

3. *The Prophet's Reluctance*

The reaction of the prophet to the realization that this was to be his life's work was not the "I will" of Isaiah or the "I won't" of Moses, but rather the "I can't" of a timid person.

Jeremiah wanted to do whatever God purposed for him, but he felt completely inadequate for the task. Placing this great responsibility alongside his own merits, he could not see how he could get the task accomplished. Two things seemed to handicap him hopelessly: his extreme youth and his lack of eloquence. Indeed, this is the usual handicap of the young man called of God. Age eventually takes care of itself, and training and experience give the poise that lies behind all eloquence. Such humility as Jeremiah reveals does not bring upon him the wrath of God. A man must not enter the ministry calmly. It is indeed a gigantic task. Humility becomes warped, however, when it keeps a man from letting God work through him. It should rather lead him to surrender to the divine strength.

4. The Enabling Power of God

The Lord reproved Jeremiah for his reluctance. Jeremiah was no longer a youth among youths, but a youth among men who must be made to listen. The secret of his success would not be his own words, but the living word of God that had been put on his tongue. The assurance "my words in thy mouth" is the guarantee of success for one who lives in the service of God. One never quite knows what to say, but the Spirit takes the Word to which one gives witness, and it does its own work of conviction or destruction. It is obvious that Jeremiah was being told what to do; this was what he needed. "Make up your own mind," is frequently a most disastrous bit of advice to a person unable to make a responsible decision. Often all he needs is someone stronger to lean upon until he gets past his complete bewilderment. Isaiah volunteered for service, but Jeremiah was drafted. God did not call him against his will, however. He helped Jeremiah do what he knew he could not face alone. Jeremiah was not overpowered; he was persuaded by one who was wiser than he. Later Jeremiah was not convinced of this, as he accused God of using undue pressure upon him (20:7), but it was a mere passing mood. He would not exchange his task for all the peace the world could offer (20:9). He knew no peace; yet dedication to divine purpose brought him closer to reality than could contentment that comes from tired surrender to difficulty.

5. *The Nature of the Ministry*

Now the ministry of Jeremiah is more clearly described. It is to be destructive in its immediate purpose but constructive in its ultimate aim. Before God can build a sound nation he must get down to rock bottom and start over again. The old plants must be uprooted and a new crop sown. One of the dilemmas of many modern churches is that those who have gone before have often laid the wrong kind of foundation. Woe to the pastor who tries to tear it out his first year on the field! Later he may get it out piece by piece, but it is a tedious process. Perhaps the most effective move is to summon a traveling evangelist who can speak out and move on!

Without some destruction there can be no real progress where men have built before. Perhaps your end of town is in the process of putting in sewers. There is considerable inconvenience until the streets are finally paved again. But how can one go forward without some inconvenience? "Let's not have any trouble," may be a suggestion from Satan instead of God. Where there is gross sin, it is better to have tension and division than to see the whole house come down upon one's head. Suppose Jeremiah had been impelled by a desire to cause no one trouble. The entrenched evil of his day would have wanted nothing better. Spurred on by God, Jeremiah kept rocking the boat, much to the dismay of the established authorities. This was not due, as is often the case, to the fact that Jeremiah had a disagreeable disposition, but to the disturbing word that God had commissioned him to deliver.

The prophet would have much preferred to live at peace with all his countrymen.

6. *The Reaffirmation of the Call*

Jeremiah was still reluctant to get started on his mission. In two impressive scenes God pressed upon him the urgency of the hour (1:11-19). In the vision of the almond branch a play on words is made in the Hebrew. The word for almond tree is *shaked,* from a root "to be awake." It is so named because it is the first tree to bloom in the spring. When Jeremiah identified the almond branch (*shaked*), God reminded him that he, too, was awake (Hebrew, *shoked*) to the world situation, and was about to act. Apparently the almond branch was not blossoming at the time, for God praised Jeremiah for his keen observation. If it had been in bloom anyone could have recognized its blossoms. Although the branch showed no sign of life, yet it would one day "awake." Only a farm lad would know a dormant almond. To the casual observer, God did not seem to care what was happening in the world. However, the man of faith could perceive that the moment for God's action was not far away. Time was short.

The other scene involved the vision of a boiling caldron that was turned toward Palestine. The literal Hebrew of 1:13 is not "the face thereof is toward the north" but rather, "the face thereof is away from the north." Someone in the north country was tipping it toward Judah. Soon the seething battle lines of Mesopotamia would move to Palestine. Time was short.

Since the end was so near, God commanded Jeremiah to arise and warn his people before it was too late (1:17*a*). They would fight him bitterly, but he must never waver lest they turn upon him (1:17*b*). This unrelenting stand would be possible because God would give the strength that he needed (1:18). There would be a terrible battle, but his

enemies would not prevail over him. Neither was Jeremiah
promised that he would prevail over them. He was promised
that he would have his opportunity to proclaim the truth.
The people could not silence him as long as God directed his
mission. They might not heed him or yield to his persuasion,
but neither would they cut him off. There must have been
times when Jeremiah doubted this, but it turned out to be
true. The greatest comfort of a God-called man is the assurance of the presence of God. Until his task is done all the
powers of hell cannot move him.

II. THE EARLY MINISTRY (2:1 to 6:30)

The urgency of Jeremiah's call experience is reflected in his
early sermons. Destruction was imminent unless Judah repented of her sins. The only hope was in forsaking her iniquity and seeking the grace of God. Many passages are
similar to those found in the book of Hosea, but Jeremiah is
always distinctive in his use of these concepts.

1. Contrast of Israel's Present with Her Past (2:1–13)

In this striking section the prophet contrasted Israel's past
faithfulness with her present infidelity. God remembered "the
kindness of thy youth, the love of thine espousals" (literally,
"the loyal love of thy youth, the love of thy honeymoon
days"). Using the figure of marriage, he recalled the first days
at Sinai when the covenant was made with Israel. His new
bride followed him out of Egypt toward a land yet unsown
with seed. Of course, trouble came before they left Sinai,
but Jeremiah emphasized the initial experiences at the holy
mountain and idealized the past. Israel was dedicated to the
Lord, and anyone who tried to harm her would have to
answer to her God (2:3).

In contrast to her early faithfulness, the bride had forsaken
her husband. Was it because her husband had been unfaith-
ful (2:5)? Of course not. Yet Israel had defiled her land, and

did not even miss the God she had abandoned (2:6). She had become like the gods she worshiped (2:5b). Jeremiah's favorite word for idol was "vanity," a word that also means nothingness, emptiness. An accurate paraphrase would be "a nobody." In seeking after "nobodies" they had become "nobodies" themselves. They did not miss the Lord because their worship of empty gods had caused them to become so degenerate that they were satisfied with the diet of nothingness the idols offered. Just so men today become so engrossed in materialistic pursuits that their shrinking souls no longer cry out for spiritual food. Such was the condition of the rich fool about whom Jesus talked.

There follows a passage that further illustrates Israel's strange unfaithfulness (2:9–13). The prophet declared that Judah's sin was worse than that of any heathen nation. It was unparalleled in the world. One might go to the isles of Chittim (Crete), as far west as possible, or to Kedar (Arabia), the eastern extreme of their world, but nothing like this could possibly be found (2:10). Although the gods that the nations worshiped were not gods at all, their worshipers remained true to them. Yet Israel, who knew the true and only God, had been persuaded to exchange her worship for profitless idolatry. Nor is the situation different today. It is a perplexing phenomenon still that the followers of materialistic philosophies or traditional idolatry rally more loyally about their gods than the typical Christian does to God.

The prophet pictured the very heavens as being horrified at such behavior: "Be astonished" (literally, "be heavy"), "and be horribly afraid" (literally, "let your hair stand on end"), "be ye very desolate" (literally, "be dried up") (2:12). The people had been guilty of two foolish sins. First, they had forsaken the Lord, who, like a fresh-flowing spring, satisfies every thirst completely. Second, for their fresh-flowing spring they had substituted cisterns of their own, which had been hewn from solid rock. It is hard to imagine that people would prefer cistern water to that of an artesian spring. Yet one continues to be amazed at the variety of tastes in people. The probable reason, however, was the fact that they had to walk some distance to the spring, whereas the cistern could be prepared in their own yard. Most people have always been tempted to follow the religion that makes the least demands upon them.

The saddest part of the whole affair turned out to be the failure of the cisterns. After having hewn them from solid rock, the people waited for the spring rains to fill them with their summer's water supply. Just as they had anticipated, the containers were soon filled to the top. Confidently they settled back to enjoy the fruits of their labor. But they had not counted upon what would happen. As the hot sun beat down upon them, the rock began to crack and the water seeped out. All their labor had been in vain! So it always happens when people try to substitute their own efforts for the gifts of God. In the hour of need they will be disappointed always. Yet the fountain keeps sending forth its water for such disillusioned souls. The life-giving flow is there yet for all who will come back to it.

2. The Nature of Sin (2:14–37)

In Jeremiah 2:14–37 the prophet vividly described two arresting characteristics of sin. First, he observed that sin is *unnatural*. The Hebrew nation had been planted as the choicest of vines, yet as the plant grew it "turned into useless suckers [turned aside things] of a strange vine to me" (2:21). The husbandman could not recognize the crop he had planted. When a man sins, he is not behaving as God created him. Sin is contrary to the original purpose of God. The moral depravity of mankind is the result of the fall. God did not so make man. Sin is a cancer upon the soul that the Great Physician must be allowed to cut out.

Second, the prophet declared that sin is *illogical*. Not only is iniquity against our original nature; indeed, it makes no sense at all. Sin contradicts every sensible thought of man. In other realms man uses his reason, but in sin he abandons it (2:31–32). If God had been a barren wasteland, one would have expected his people to leave him. Instead he had been the source of life. It made no sense that they would desert him.

If God had been darkness, it could be understood why his people made their own light. The truth, however, is that he is the source of light. Why did they consider themselves self-sufficient? It is beyond comprehension.

A young girl can never forget that she is wearing her new jewelry, nor a bride her trousseau. Yet Israel had lost all consciousness of her chief source for glorying—her God. Israel's only claim to superiority was her religion. When she lost that, her boasting became unreasonable.

The Christian way of life is the only sensible way. Some have considered the teachings of the Sermon on the Mount to be an ideal for the future. Such it is; but it is more than that. It is the only practical way for man to live now if he would live happily in human society. Its principles are not a luxury but a necessity. It is sin that makes no sense for the practical minded.

If sin is both unnatural and illogical, why do men become involved in it? Jeremiah suggests three motives.

(1) *Men turn to sin in rebellion against restraint.*—They consider the laws of God too demanding, too stringent. As God was leading his people, they found the going too hard, green pastures too appealing (2:17–18). They had thrown off the divine restraint: "For of old time you have broken your yoke, you have burst your reins" (literal Hebrew 2:20).

Just so, people continue to reject religion today because they think it demands more self-denial than they are willing to exercise. What they fail to realize is that only as one lets

God help him control himself can he attain any worthy objectives. Broken loose on his own, the rebellious animal will only tear himself upon a barbed-wire fence. Men continue to marvel at the foolishness of Esau, who sold his birthright for a mess of pottage. Yet they continue to do the same. They leave one master only to be enslaved by another.

(2) *Desire to satisfy sinful lusts.* A second motive that leads men into sin is the desire to satisfy the lusts of the flesh. Here was the real appeal of Baalism. This religion taught that the fertility of the land was brought about by the union of male and female gods. This could be guaranteed by sexual relations with persons dedicated to these gods. What chance existed for a morally demanding religion when faced with such an alternative (2:20)? Israel is likened to a wild ass in heat that races to find a mate (2:24–25). Christianity is meant only for those who want what it guarantees. The man who prefers the flesh, and thereby destruction of his own soul, must lie in the bed he has made.

(3) *Love of money.*—A third motive for sin is the love of money. There is no crime that men will not commit to get the money they think they need. This has become all too clear in our country. In the prophet's day the poor were being sacrificed upon the altar of the rich (2:34). Innocent men were being exploited without cause. A man bent on satisfying his own whims will allow nothing to stand in his way. What does he care for the poor except as they will add to his wealth? A money-mad age is not interested in the rights of men.

3. *The Consequences of Sin* (2:14–37)

If a man is so foolish as to choose sin, he must bear its consequences. Jeremiah notes three of these.

(1) *Sin brings misery to the sinner* (2:14–17).—As a consequence of her sin Israel's land lay waste, her cities depopulated. All of this she had brought upon herself. Sin brings its

own judgment with it. Once the forces are set in action, the result is assured.

(2) *Sin always disappoints.*—God leaves the sinner to his own resources (2:28). If a man is to meet the crises of life, he needs to walk with God every day. Unless contact is continual, sudden emergencies may arise when there is no time for the elimination of static. Faith, like treasure, must be stored up for a rainy day.

(3) *Sin tends to blind a man to his true condition.*—One of the tragic results of sin, however, is that it, like all forms of insanity, tends to blind a man to his true condition, thus making it more and more difficult for him to repent. How can one repent who sees nothing wrong with himself (2:23a,30,35)? People tell their minister that they like for him to preach against their sins. What they mean is that they appreciate sermons condemning what they already know to be wrong. Yet whenever a preacher points out as sin something in which they see nothing wrong, they are ready to tar and feather him. The most awful fact about sin is that even while the sinner is racing madly for hell, he rides merrily along thinking that paradise is his destination.

Finally, Jeremiah reminded his hearers that no amount of outward reform could change sin's consequences (2:22). Sin is more than skin deep. Any cure for its sickness must be applied to the heart, not the skin. Nothing applied to the outside of the body can effect the salvation of the soul. This includes the water of baptism, for it can only signify what has already taken place in the heart.

4. *Hope for the Hopeless* (3:1 to 4:4)

Some scholars contend that Jeremiah was a prophet without hope. Yet in this section there is a vivid example of his extending hope to the most desperate of backsliders. To those who think they have sinned past redemption, these passages still offer the boon of forgiveness. The fact that such assurance of a merciful God comes from the fiercest prophet of divine wrath is all the more encouraging.

As Jeremiah described the condition of the people throughout this section, it is apparent that their state could not have been worse. They had given themselves completely to idolatry and immorality (3:2). They had even lost the ability to blush; nothing shamed them (3:3). They presumed upon the grace of God, thinking that like a doting earthly father, after a while he would change his mood and overlook their disobedience (3:4–5). They did not realize that he would never change his mind about them until they changed their way of living. Because of what God is, he must punish sin. Kinship ties are not enough to assure safety from his wrath.

The worst aspect of their sin was that it was committed in face of the evident love of God (3:19–20). God had purposed to make them his sons and give them a blessed inheritance, but by their faithlessness they had thwarted his purpose for them. Instead they turned to "the multitude of mountains" (3:23). The word "multitude" is literally "orgies." The loud orgies of the pagan fertility cults could be heard for miles around. There was something tragic about it, however, for it was only a vain attempt to drown out the voice of their God-given conscience. This sad scene is obviously being repeated in the harsh jazz of our own times.

Finally, the Israelites' state had become so wretched that even they realized its shamefulness and turned to God for help (3:22b,24–25). Yet as they came to him, they were only conscious of their unworthiness and hopelessness. Sin had them helpless in its grip, for traditional sins are even more difficult to conquer than personal ones. They must overcome not only their own sins, but also what had been handed down to them by their fathers. They must overturn the weight of centuries of influence. Could anything be done for them? It was certain that they could do nothing to help themselves.

Still there was God. Would he be willing to help them after all that they had done? It is so difficult for a wretched sinner to believe this. A man would not be likely to take back a wife he had divorced, after she had married another (3:1). Yet the Lord will take back his people after they have been separated from him. Whenever they truly desire to leave their new loves and return to an intimate walk with their true husband, God will take them back (4:1). This verse could be paraphrased: "If you want to return, you can return; if you put away your abominations out of my sight, then you can quit your wandering." The verb "to wander" is the root of the noun "vagabond," used of Cain in Genesis 4:12,14. God not only will receive the penitent backsliders; he will *cure* their sinful waywardness (3:22). The success of the surrendered life is assured by God himself. For him not to see such a person through to the end would either mean he was unable or untrue. It is inconceivable that either alternative could characterize the sovereign God.

When once the wayward sinners are wholly surrendered to God, the divine purpose will be realized through them (4:2). They will experience the truth, justice, and righteousness of God. Unbelievers will see God at work in the believers and be drawn to an experience with him. Thus the nations will be won to God, not by some miraculous blow from the Lord, but by the living testimony of the changed lives of his people.

5. The Oracles of Doom (4:5 to 6:30)

Scattered throughout this section are lyric poems describing the imminent invasion of a mysterious foe from the north. What nation did Jeremiah have in mind? There are many opinions.[1] Some scholars say that he was thinking of the Scythians, a primitive people who terrorized the whole

---

[1] Cf. James Philip Hyatt, "The Book of Jeremiah," *The Interpreter's Bible* (Nashville: Abingdon Press, 1956), V, 779b.

region at some time during this period. They had rushed to the aid of Assyria from their home in the Caucasian steppes of what is modern Russia. Others suggest that he meant Babylon. Probably he had no particular nation in mind at first. He only knew that the destruction was soon to come. Josiah's reforms delayed this, and Jeremiah remained quiet until the king's death. It was then that it became quite plain to the prophet that the nation would be Babylon. As he dictated to Baruch, this would naturally color the wording of the final recording of the oracles.

Imbedded in this section of desperate warnings are two passages of particular interest. In 5:1-6 we are told of Jeremiah's frantic attempts to save Jerusalem. If he could find a single man who honestly sought truth, and who, after finding it, tried to do something about it, the city could be delivered. First, the prophet searched for such a man among the common people. To his dismay, he discovered that the more they had suffered under the corrective hand of God, the more stubbornly they had rebelled against him.

Perhaps, the prophet said to himself, this was due to the fact that they were not aware of the ways of God with men. They had not been taught enough to recognize what God was trying to say to them (5:4). If he went to those who had been educated and taught in the revelation of God, he would get a better reception (v. 5a). Indeed, he discovered that they were well aware of what God expected, yet they had flagrantly and openly rebelled against his known will. Nothing was left but sure and certain destruction (5:6).

The other passage concerns the possibility of reconciliation if there is a change of heart. Jeremiah kept hoping against hope. Yet his efforts were fruitless even in the turn of events reflected in the Josianic reforms. This oracle (6:16-21) called upon the people to stop their mad rush to ruin. Standing at the crossroads of the future they were to inquire concerning the proper road to take. Specifically they were to ask for the "old paths" (literally, "deep-rutted roads of old"), the roads that had been traveled so frequently that once one was on them, he could not lose his way. Yet it was not enough that the road be old and much used. Just because it was old, it does not necessarily mean that it was the proper one. From among the various oft-traveled paths, they were to inquire concerning which of them was the good one—the one that would get them where they wanted to go. Of course, they had to be careful to whom they put the question; else the right answer might not be forthcoming (6:17). If they would take the time-honored road of faith and surrender to God, they would find rest (literally, "quiet") for their souls.

To Jeremiah's plea, however, the people turned a deaf ear. They refused to walk the old paths plainly pointed out by divine revelation. Rather they insisted upon their headlong rush after their own desires. Into their path God would place stumbling blocks (6:21), and they would never achieve the goal for which they strove.

In these days of the high-speed expressways, it is even more difficult to persuade people to take the old road. Yet it remains the only path that leads home. All others simply hasten men on the road to nowhere.

FOR STUDY AND DISCUSSION

1. Ask your pastor to describe his call to preach. See if you can detect its influence on the sermons you have heard him preach.
2. What keeps men from answering God's call today? What would he say to them?
3. What are some "broken cisterns" that people rely upon?
4. Describe the sins peculiar to your own community. What can be done about them?
5. Do we have "a foe from the north"? Who might it be?

CHAPTER 3 OUTLINE

I. THE OCCASION (7:1–16; 26:1–24)
   1. Temple Superstition
   2. Opposition of the Priests and the Prophets
   3. The Defense of Jeremiah
   4. The Contrast with Uriah

II. THE SERMON (7:1 to 8:3)
   1. The Rebel Prophet
   2. The Destruction of Externals
   3. What Is Left? (3:17–18)
   4. The New Externals (33:10–26)

3

The Temple Sermon

7:1 to 8:3; 26:1–24

ONE OF THE GREATEST SERMONS, if not the greatest, in the Old Testament is to be studied in this chapter. It contains the heart of the message of Jeremiah, who was himself all heart. It is this passage that lies behind the words used by Jesus when he cleansed the Temple (cf. Matt. 21:13 with Jer. 7:11). Here is recorded in the immortal words of a tortured soul the true nature of religion: It is a personal walk with God. In stark contrast to this is the mistaken concept of the average man that essential religion consists of loyalty to the institutions set up by religionists. Jeremiah insisted that these institutions have value in their proper place, but the temptation to substitute them for a valid experience with God is fatal both to the worshiper and the institution.

I. THE OCCASION (7:1–16; 26:1–24)

In the early part of Jehoiakim's reign, when the people had gathered at the Temple for a special feast day, Jeremiah delivered these scathing words. Great throngs were there making their offerings to God, and the well-trained choirs were chanting their liturgies. Yet something was tragically wrong.

1. Temple Superstition

The chanting of the choirs was in perfect harmony, but it grated upon the prophet's ears. It was not in tune with the divine Word. "The temple of the Lord, The temple of the Lord, The temple of the Lord, are these [buildings]," they sang (7:4), implying that because this was so, they were

37

safe from all harm. Before anyone could capture the Temple
and the Holy City, they thought he must first of all defeat
the One whose possession it was. Of course this was impossible, so Jerusalem was safe from every attack.

This comforting doctrine had come to prevail in Judah
because of a misunderstanding of the prophecies of Isaiah.
When the city of Jerusalem was under attack by the Assyrian
king Sennacherib, the invader had brazenly challenged the
living God (Isa. 36:18–20). Isaiah arose to the occasion to
announce that God would dramatically dispose of the rash
braggart (Isa. 37:29). When the crisis should be over, Jerusalem would be established as the Lord's throne forever (Isa.
33:20), its stakes never to be pulled up by a foreign invader.
The people of Jeremiah's day naturally concluded that the
city of which Isaiah was speaking was their own Jerusalem,
which accordingly could never fall. It was too dear to the
Lord. "How mistaken you are!" cried Jeremiah. "You are
trusting in lying words when you sing 'the temple of the
Lord.'" The Temple was inviolate only so long as the people
were true to the Lord. Obedience had always been more
important than sacrifice. Isaiah had been speaking of the
ideal city of God in Isaiah 33:20, not the present one. Not
until its people truly belonged to God could their place of
worship be secure.

In fact, it was evident that such was not the case in Judah.
All the commandments of God were being broken (Jer. 7:9).
Yet the people thought that they could commit such crime
and be acceptable to God as long as they attended the
Temple services and brought their offerings. Thus the Temple had become a den of robbers, a place to which they could
flee and find safety from the wrath of God. This Temple,
whose ritual had become a substitute for morality, was as
doomed as the one at Shiloh. This first temple was supervised by Eli (1 Sam. 1–4), and likewise was the center of

the worship of the true God. Eli's sons, however, cared nothing for the moral demands of God. By taking the ark of God into battle against the Philistines, they thought it would guarantee a victory for their side. Instead, even to the surprise of the Philistines, the ark itself was captured. Although no accounts of the events are preserved in the Old Testament, it is certain that in the conflicts that followed, the Philistines also destroyed Shiloh, for in the days of David the sacrificing priests were no longer serving there (1 Sam. 21:1).

Jeremiah used this well-known event in history to prove that no place is so sacred to God that it cannot be destroyed when the people who congregate there defy the wrath of God. Unless they repented of all their wickedness, those who frequented the Temple would feel the heavy hand of God's judgment: "I will make this house like Shiloh, and will make this city a curse to all the nations of the earth" (Jer. 26:6).

2. *Opposition of the Priests and the Prophets*

Listening to Jeremiah preach were the religious leaders of Jerusalem, who had been telling people that all was well between Israel and God. As long as they came to worship and brought their sacrifices, they had nothing to fear. The Lord would soon act to destroy all the enemies of the Hebrews and cause the nations to come bowing before them. What Jeremiah was preaching was blatant heresy, they said. Had not Solomon declared when he built the Temple, "I have surely built thee an house to dwell in, a settled place for thee to abide in for ever" (1 Kings 8:13)? And had not the great Isaiah prophesied that Zion never would fall (Isa. 33:20)? They were quite convinced that Jeremiah was deceived. Besides, if he was right, they were wrong, and their prestige among the people would suffer. It was a simple matter for them to incite the people into a mob ready to lynch the heretic. Notice the order in Jeremiah 26:8. Jeremiah had been addressing the people primarily, but the priests and prophets took the leadership in the response, and the people followed along after them.

3. *The Defense of Jeremiah*

Soon the word reached the princes of Judah concerning the disorder in the Temple courts, and they appeared to hear the case. In Old Testament days, court was held in the gate of the Temple in Jerusalem. These nobles had grown up under Josiah and represented the godly leaders of that era. Their place would soon be taken over by the picked friends of Jehoiakim; but during the early part of Jehoiakim's reign, they were still in power.

Formal accusation was made by the priests and prophets, while the princes and people listened (26:11). Jeremiah had been guilty of blasphemy, for he had condemned God's chosen city. To them there was no difference between this and condemning God himself. Established religious authorities are always prone to commit this error. A word against an institution is a word against God. A member of a church arose to say in a business meeting: "The pastor should never be criticized by the people. As long as he is pastor, he is to be respected and agreed with." In his opinion, to criticize the pastor amounted to questioning God. This was never meant to be. Of course, there is no place for littleness and bickering between a layman and his minister. However, being a minister himself, the author knows how wrong it would be to follow one blindly. The people share the responsibility of testing the words of their leader against the Word of God. However, they are ill equipped to do so, unless other leaders give the other side.

That was what happened in the Temple. First Jeremiah spoke. The words he had uttered were not out of his own imagination. He had been sent by God to warn them that unless they changed their ways they were doomed (26:12–13). Aware that he was in danger of losing his life, he could but speak what he had been commanded to say. He placed himself in their hands, to do with him as they would. If they took his life, they were adding more innocent blood to their previous crimes, and they, in turn, would find themselves in the hands of God, who would do with them what he would (26:14–15).

Immediately the princes saw that Jeremiah had a strong case. The people, who had blindly followed their leaders, had not heard the other side, and also now saw that Jeremiah had committed no crime. (It is a conviction of the author that the average congregation will not make poor decisions except when only one side of the picture is given them. If they can be helped to see all the alternatives clearly, they can be relied upon to do the right thing.)

Soon certain elders spoke out in Jeremiah's defense, citing the case of the prophet Micah, who had prophesied a hundred years before! He, too, had said that Jerusalem would be destroyed. But did Hezekiah put him to death? Of course not. Rather, he turned to God, heeding the prophet, and thus the city was saved. If they killed Jeremiah, they could be making a great mistake. The man who was most influential in saving Jeremiah was Ahikam, the son of Shaphan (26:24). The scribe Shaphan and his son Ahikam were leaders in the reform of Josiah (2 Kings 22), and were no doubt quite alarmed over the turn that Jehoiakim's reign had taken.

4. The Contrast with Uriah

A footnote to the Temple sermon episode is quite instructive (26:20–23). It tells the story of the prophet Uriah, who also prophesied that Jerusalem would be destroyed. When Jehoiakim heard about it, he was determined to destroy Uriah, who had no friends at court, as did Jeremiah. Hearing of his imminent danger, Uriah fled in fear to Egypt, but he was brought by force back to Judah, summarily executed, and denied a decent burial.

What is the point of this story? Apparently it is meant to underscore the difference between these two men. They both delivered the word given them by God, but whereas Jeremiah stood his ground afterward, Uriah fled for his life. In his original call Jeremiah had been told, "Be not dismayed at their faces, lest I confound thee before them" (1:17). The true prophet does not speak and run away. He speaks and takes his stand. It is the stand that seals the prophecy. It demonstrates that one not only is making a speech; he is so sure that God is in the word that he will back it up with his life. There is no defense for the prophet who speaks and runs away. Why should he flee to Egypt when the arms of God are already about him?

II. The Sermon (7:1 to 8:3)

Having examined the setting in which the sermon was given, let us look more closely at the message itself, for its truths are as applicable for today as when they were first uttered.

1. The Rebel Prophet

One writer has aptly named his study of Jeremiah *The Rebel Prophet*.[1] No term could better describe him:

A rebel! What scorn and hatred lie behind the stigma! The last and cruellest word that a man can fling at his foe, Rebel. With this for his surname, no man may lift his face to his fellows, for every man's hand is against him. Those strong social instincts that beat in the breast of every friendly man rise up in blinded fury to crush the man who defies convention. Society is held together by laws and customs, by habits and etiquettes, and when these are challenged or defied the life of society is im-

---

[1] T. Crouther Gordon, *The Rebel Prophet* (New York: Harper & Brothers, 1932).

perilled. By a strange unreasoning instinct the social consciousness knows the rebel to be its deadliest foe, and singles him out
for martyrdom. And society is right. If all were rebels the social
unit would disappear. Thus society hates the defiant individual
with a terrible hatred, a hatred unrelieved by mercy. It heaps
upon the exceptional man its vilest stigma and crowns him
with the terrible curse of loneliness. It plies him with every
weapon, from social ostracism to the hangman's rope, drawn
from its vast and cavernous armoury.[2]

Gordon goes on to observe that rebels are of two sorts.
One variety refuses to go along with progress and keeps
pulling back when others want to go ahead. Such men are
more concerned with their own selfish ways than the good
of society. These are our criminals or "our contemporary ancestors." The other sort, however, is represented by Jeremiah. He is not the man who lags behind, but the one who
is ahead of all the others. He rebels because he cares for
others and wants to save them from themselves. The sad
fact is that society treats both kinds of men alike.

2. The Destruction of Externals

The point of Jeremiah's sermon was that all the externals
that the Israelites thought were necessary to their religion
would soon be destroyed, because these had become substi-
tutes for God. Their institutions had come between them
and God and, as a consequence, had to go.

(1) The ark would be destroyed.—The destruction of the
ark is taken for granted in Jeremiah 3:16. Not only would it
be lost, but the people would not even need it or remember
it. How could this ever be? The ark was the symbol of the
presence of God. Since the days of the wilderness journeys
it had been the rallying point of the worship of Israel. In it
were stored samples of the manna, Aaron's rod that budded,
and the stones bearing the Ten Commandments. As someone has said, it was Israel's Museum of Supernatural History.

[2] Ibid., p. 88.

It was so precious in the sight of God that the Philistine god fell broken before it (1 Sam. 5:1 ff.) and a careless hand touching it meant certain destruction (2 Sam. 6:7). How could Israel get along without the ark? Yet Jeremiah claimed that not only would the Hebrews lose the ark in the Babylonian disaster, but also the time would come when there would be no need for it.

(2) *The Temple would go.*—Along with the ark would go the Temple. Since the days of Solomon this structure had housed the ark and was the focal area of the religion of Judah. After the fall of Samaria it became central for all Israel. Around Zion gathered all the future hope of Israel (Isa. 2:1 ff.). Jerusalem was God's dwelling place upon earth. Here alone could sacrifice be made, and sacrifice was at the core of the Lord's demands. To be away from Jerusalem was to know only sorrow and heartache. Psalm 137 graphically pictures the common attitude toward exile: "How shall we sing the Lord's song in a strange land? If I forget thee, O Jerusalem, let my right hand forget her cunning. If I do not remember thee, let my tongue cleave to the roof of my mouth; if I prefer not Jerusalem above my chief joy" (Psalm 137:4–6). It was a city to be loved above all cities, to be defended at any cost from all who would attack it. To lose it would mean to relinquish all the promises of God to defend his own. In the Talmud the rabbis said that a Jew away from his land was like a man without a god. Yet Jeremiah declared that the Temple would be destroyed.

(3) *The sacrificial system would cease.*—With the destruction of the Temple would come the cessation of the sacrificial system, for it was inseparably linked with the Temple itself. The teachings of Jeremiah about sacrifice are matters of great dispute among scholars and deserve some attention at this point. The more liberal scholars have long contended that Jeremiah 7:21–23 can mean nothing except that Jeremiah was saying that Moses had nothing to do with sacrifice.

At Sinai the covenant of the law was given, but the sacrificial system was a later adaptation of Canaanite practices and never had the approval of God.[3] This is their position in spite of the abundant evidence elsewhere to the contrary. Modern scholars are tending more to other explanations of the difficult passage.[4]

Either of two explanations would agree with the claims elsewhere that the basic sacrificial system had divine approval from the time of Moses. One would suggest that the phrase closing Jeremiah 7:22, rather than reading "concerning burnt offerings or sacrifices," should read "for the sake of burnt offerings and sacrifices." Let the people continue to bring their offerings and eat their portions in the sacred precincts of the temple (7:21). This they loved to do, for the meat was the very best. But let them remember that God did not command sacrifice for the sake of being fed himself (7:22), but rather as a test of their obedience. The heathen believed that their gods actually partook of their sacrifices and lived upon them.[5] If they obey in bringing sacrifice but omit the weightier matters, they have sorely misunderstood the covenant!

The other suggestion is to emphasize "in the day" in 7:22. The first day that they arrived at Sinai (the day they finished coming out of Egypt) God instituted the covenant of obedience (Ex. 19:1-9). It was not until later that sacrifice was regulated. Therefore primacy is to be placed upon obedience, because it was given first place. The passage teaches, therefore, that obedience is better than sacrifice.

(4) *Israel would cease as a nation.*—The worst blow of all, however, was that the covenant at Sinai would be an-

---

[3] George Adam Smith, *Jeremiah* (New York: Harper & Brothers, 1929), pp. 156–159.

[4] H. H. Rowley, *The Re-Discovery of the Old Testament* (Philadelphia: The Westminster Press, 1946), pp. 154–159.

[5] *Enuma Elish* (Babylonia Creation Epic), Tablet VI, lines 109–120.

nulled. Israel would cease as a nation. Until now the Sinai covenant had preserved Judah's hope for the future. When Israel fell in 722 B.C., it was quite a blow to Hebrew optimism, but Judah carried on the great tradition. It was believed that through her the promises of the universal rule of Israel would be achieved. Now Jeremiah was preaching that the end of the nation of Judah was at hand. Since the nation had not obeyed the voice of God (7:28), it had broken the covenant. The Lord had "forsaken the generation of his wrath" (7:29). The nation as a political unit would cease to exist, for God was saying that he would leave the entire land desolate after the outpouring of his wrath (7:34). Such a fate for Jerusalem was beyond the comprehension of Jeremiah's contemporaries. All their hope in the future had been built around their nation. It was with the nation that the Sinai covenant was made, and it was the nation that gave meaning to the individual. His principal hope for immortality was in the future of Israel itself. With the nation destroyed, how could God possibly find a way to accomplish his purpose, for the nation was his chosen vessel?

This matter is still being debated among Jews today. The leaders of the nation of Israel are saying that the future of the Jews is inseparably linked with the political state. Others, particularly American Jews who prefer the United States as their country, are contending that it is their common heritage, quite independent of political affiliation, that holds them together. Since the debate has continued over two thousand years, it is no wonder that Jeremiah found his contemporaries difficult to convince. God would see them through their crisis, they thought, as he had done before. Because the Temple never had been destroyed, they thought it never could be demolished. They little realized that God had a purpose in history and that the past was no guarantee of the future. Time runs out on both individuals and nations. The patience of God is often confused with a lack of concern on his part. The fact that he has not judged sin is not due to his indifference to what is going on, but rather to his long-suffering. Man must not presume upon this, as did Israel.

3. *What Is Left?* (3:17–18)

After Jeremiah had announced that the ark of the covenant would not even be missed, the question would naturally be asked, "If the Temple, the ark, and the nation cease to exist, what do we have left? Is not that the end of our religion?" "Why, no," the prophet replied. "In the grace of God, all that he has ever purposed will yet come to pass without the externals you find so necessary today. The people of Judah and Israel will return from exile, and Jerusalem will become the center of the life of the world. Not only will the hearts of all the people be changed, but also Judah and Israel shall learn to live together in peace and unity." What is left? To that question Jeremiah replied, "Everything is left that is essential to the survival of the true faith." And what is that? "The living God and a remnant who know God." If the remnant is destroyed, nothing is left. If the institutions are destroyed, the surviving and disciplined remnant will one day rebuild the wasteland.

How had Jeremiah come to see this? Of course, God had revealed it to him, but why had he not revealed it to someone else also? It had come to Jeremiah out of his own experience and need. God gives an answer to those who need and seek it. Jeremiah needed an answer desperately, and he knew where to go to get it. During his early ministry he had seen one of the noblest attempts at religious reform undertaken. Josiah had revitalized every institution dear to the Hebrew heart. Yet no permanent results came from it. It did not reach the inner motivation of people. They simply obeyed their king without question. When a new king, Jehoiakim, came to the throne and led in the opposite direction, they followed him just as faithfully away from God.

Somehow outward reform could not achieve the permanent purpose of God.

It was in his own personal experience that Jeremiah came to grasp the deepest truths. When he began to proclaim faithfully what God had said to him, he found himself shut off from all society and approved forms of public worship. What was left for him? His own personal experience with God; that was everything. Religion to him was an affair of the heart, a matter of inward experience. The reason why Jeremiah knew that if all externals were destroyed everything would not be lost was the testimony of his own life. God had already told him that the institutions dear to his own soul as well as to the others must go. Already he had asked the question, "What then is left?" And God had given the clear answer, "God and the man of faith."

Men have always thought that when institutions and ways of expressing faith have changed, religion itself was dying. Many times, however, that was not what was really happening. A living faith had found it necessary to move in a way that was needful to a new generation. The Hebrews of Jeremiah's day could not imagine life without the Temple, yet when it actually was destroyed, they discovered that the local congregation could worship effectively without either a Temple or sacrifice. The synagogue worship was not discontinued even after the Temple was rebuilt. Judaism through the destruction of the old externals had found a new way of life.

The Jewish Christians in New Testament times found it difficult to live without the rules that had been taught them from boyhood. So convinced were they of their necessity that they tried to force their peculiarities upon the new Gentile Christians. The tension became so great that the Jerusalem conference had to be held (Acts 15). Yet soon the churches left all these Jewish practices behind and no one was the loser. The new faith had found its own best expression.

In the Reformation devout Roman Catholics could not imagine how the new Protestants could survive without the pope, the confessional, purgatory, or the veneration of the Virgin Mary. Yet these same churches have done quite well for themselves without those forms to which they had been accustomed and have developed institutions that reflect their own particular emphases.

When modern Baptists organized their churches, they would have nothing of the liturgy and forms of the established churches. They insisted upon the complete independence of the local church from hierarchic control, and a natural expression of a vital faith. How can they ever survive, others thought, without some governing body or common creed? Yet with the Bible as their only authoritative guide, Southern Baptists have a record of co-operation among their independent churches that is a challenge to more closely knit denominations. As a free people, searching for and developing new ways of expressing themselves, they have built their own distinctive institutions.

There is not one of us who would not fight for these institutions so dear to us and so necessary to the survival of our faith in today's world. Yet all of us must be prepared for what may be ahead. An atomic war (God forbid that it should ever come!) could wipe out every institution that we possess. Would this mean the death of our faith? Of course not. It might mean that we would have eight million less members, but the remnant that was left would devise the latest methods to meet the challenge of the new age.

4. *The New Externals* (33:10–26)

Jeremiah was led to show just this in the chapter under consideration. After the destruction of the Temple and the nation, the people would learn that these were not central in their faith but were its valid forms. When they had learned their proper place, then God would permit them to be restored. Temple and sacrifice would begin again. As certain as the rising of the sun was the restoration of the externals of the faith (33:19–29). This is so strange a statement coming from the prophet of the heart that some scholars question his authorship of these passages.[6] Yet the verses are carefully dated and assigned to him (33:1,19). One must not decide beforehand what a prophet should say. One must try to understand what he says. Jeremiah had never been opposed to the Temple or sacrifice or the nation. He loved them all and saw their necessity in their proper place. Later the restored exiles discovered that Jeremiah was right. They could not respond properly as a people to the leadership of God without a Temple and a city around which to rally. The time would come when the Temple and sacrifice would no longer be necessary, but it was not yet.

It was the responsibility of Haggai and Zechariah to encourage the Israelites to rebuild the Temple after the Exile. By this time they had become so accustomed to worshiping without a Temple that they saw no immediate need for one (Haggai 1:2). In fact, persuading them was such a difficult task that for the only time in Hebrew history two canonical prophets were called to work together as a team! Usually the prophets served alone, even if they were contemporaries (cf. Isaiah and Micah, Amos and Hosea, Jeremiah and Ezekiel).

Jeremiah was called not only to destroy, but also to build and to plant (Jer. 1:10). However, he had little opportunity to do the latter. He could only state his conviction that the Temple would be restored. Without such assurances from the prophet of divine wrath, the returned exiles might have used his denunciations as an excuse for neglecting the Tem-

---

[6] Cf. John Skinner, *Prophecy and Religion* (Cambridge: The University Press, 1948), pp. 310–311.

ple's rebuilding. Instead, his predictions of restoration became their chief source of confidence that the rebuilding must take place (Dan. 9:2; 2 Chron. 36:21 ff.).

FOR STUDY AND DISCUSSION

1. What are some ways that Christianity is expressed today that would have seemed strange to people one hundred years ago? Is the music used in worship different? Why?
2. Can you think of any new expression that Baptists should give to their beliefs? Do we have too many institutions or not enough?
3. Is there any danger today that form may be substituted for personal religion? How can this be guarded against?
4. Are you an independent thinker or a conformist? Which would you prefer to be? Why?

CHAPTER 4 OUTLINE

I. FALSE WISDOM
1. Wisdom Confused with Knowledge of the Law (8:8–13)
2. Wisdom Confused with Humanistic Philosophy (10:1–16)

II. TRUE WISDOM
1. Recognizes the Inability of Man to Direct Himself (8:14–22; 10:23–24)
2. Found Only in Knowledge of God (9:23–24)
3. Perceives the Signs of the Times (9:12–22; 10:17–22)

III. THE FOOLISHNESS OF ISRAEL (8:4–7)

4

False and True Wisdom

In Jeremiah 8–10 is found a collection of the prophet's sayings on wisdom, which date from various periods of his ministry. To the Hebrews true wisdom was never thought to be merely intellectual but was concerned with the practical aspects of an understanding of the true nature of society and the world. Such knowledge could not be possessed by anyone who did not comprehend the ways of God. God's righteous laws constituted the character of the universe; true wisdom would lead a man to live his own life in accordance with the divine pattern. Such wisdom could not be learned from men but only through revelation from God.

I. False Wisdom

The prophet deals with two kinds of wisdom that miss the mark. The first kind is one that particularly plagues religious communities, and the other is the tendency of the natural man.

1. *Wisdom Confused with Knowledge of the Law* (8:8–13)

Israel thought that because she had the law of God, she was wise (8:8). Yet those who knew the law best, the scribes, had twisted the law to make it mean whatever they wanted. The expression "the pen of the scribes is in vain" (8:8) should be translated "the pen of the scribes is in falsehood." That meant that the scribes had given the law a meaning never intended by God when he gave it. They

53

saw only peace for Israel in the Torah and would not apply its curses (8:11).

This is still the Christian's greatest dilemma. Although he knows that the Bible is the Word of God, yet, as he reads it, how can he be sure that he hears what God is saying to him rather than what his own teachers have pointed out? We tend to read into a passage our own prejudices and preconceived notions. We speak to the text and receive back from it our own voice rather than the word of God. When the author was growing up, he became exasperated over how church literature sometimes dealt with problems of scriptural interpretation over which the various denominations disagreed. The Baptist position would be stated and the text expounded that proved the Baptist position. The verses that were being used by the other side by the church around the corner would be completely ignored, as we pretended they were not in the Bible. And the neighboring church was doing the same thing with its own little set of proof-texts. If an honest searching of the Scriptures will not lead a person to the Baptist position, then we do well to re-examine our own views. Of all people Baptists should listen to the clear Word of God rather than the voice of their own human traditions. This is what our forefathers did as they dared to follow the Bible wherever it led them. We must not let their voices drown out the divine call that comes to us as God continues to speak to us beyond what they could hear; else we are not their true followers.

Yet this is difficult to do. It is much easier for the average person to accept what he is taught without question than to find his own way under God. The water is deep, and the fear comes that he may drown. Nevertheless, beneath him will be the everlasting arms. Even as we honestly try to let God speak to us from the Scriptures, we often mistake the voice that responds.

Some years ago a book was written by a missionary of

another denomination. During World War II he had been seized and placed in a concentration camp. His only book was the Bible. With this as his constant companion he spent his years of imprisonment. Becoming particularly interested in the book of Leviticus, he prayed and studied, and prayed even more for understanding. A commentary resulted, which he claimed was written with the help of the Holy Spirit alone. Yet as one reads the book, he must plainly doubt the statement. Every page reveals that he was helplessly dependent upon the teachers who had trained him in his denomination's schools before he became a missionary. He had confused the ghosts of their voices with the Spirit of God.

Why does the Presbyterian read his New Testament and remain a Presbyterian? He is honest and sincere, but he just cannot discover the Baptist position there. What keeps a devout Methodist still of the conviction that he may yet be lost, when to the Baptist such a thought is inconceivable as he reads his Bible? Just as sincerely as we, they search the Scriptures for divine truth, yet the Bible continues to give them the answer of their own tradition. How, then, can we be sure that we have the truth? May we not also be deluding ourselves?

Unless we face this very real possibility, we can never hear God speak. Until we are willing to leave all and follow him, we really never can hear his voice. Once we have made the plunge and have opened our minds, we will discover that our forefathers were right in their Baptist position, but we will be convinced, not because we were taught so, but because we, too, have heard God speak. As he speaks to this new generation, the truth will come out fresh, bringing us a new understanding beyond that of those who have gone before. God's Word does not change, but our understanding of it should continue to grow. The truth is there, ever to be sought, and forever beyond our final comprehension.

To possess the law does not guarantee that one knows

what it means, Jeremiah was saying. The Jews had received it but could not interpret it. The man who has read the Bible through ten times may not know how to interpret it.

A man taught an adult men's class in a church. He was regarded as an excellent teacher. The strange thing about him, however, was that he had never joined any church! To class members he was a great teacher because he could tell the Bible stories effectively and was delightfully entertaining. He knew the subject matter of the Bible, but it had not reached his personal life. He possessed the Word, but it had not possessed him. We must constantly guard against using the Bible for our own purposes, even unconsciously, and dedicate ourselves to living out its demands upon us.

2. Wisdom Confused with Humanistic Philosophy (10:1-16)

Jeremiah said that the nations did not recognize the law of God at all but depended upon their own ideas for knowledge. They created their own gods, then bowed down to worship them. What stupidity! They went into the forest and cut down a tree, and decorated it with silver and gold. It could not speak or move about, yet it became a god. What was subject to man's will became his own master (10:1-9).

Verse 11 is in Aramaic rather than Hebrew. In the midst of a book where every passage is in Hebrew, why is one statement in another language? Evidently the Jews of the exile used this verse extensively and taught it to their children to protect them from following the idols of the people among whom they lived. Aramaic was the common language of the period of the exile. Every time Gentiles tried to persuade an Israelite to turn to idolatry, he would reply with this statement in their own language.

In contrast with helpless idols, the God of Israel is a living God. He is the King of the nations (10:7,10). It is he who made the heavens and the earth and rules over them

(10:12–13). Compared to his wisdom, the knowledge of man is insignificant (10:14). It is to his people that he gives his wisdom. No one else can discover it (10:16).

Today few people are tempted to follow after the sort of idolatry that Jeremiah was battling, but just as great is the temptation to make the work of their own hands into their gods. They do not come to an actual temple dedicated to their gods, or bring in sacrifices, yet they are just as much the slaves of the work of their hands. The phrase from Jeremiah "For the customs of the people are vain" (10:3) could be translated "Man's ways are false." This is just as true today as it was in the last days of Judah.

Men who fail to acknowledge the revelation of God must try to find their own way, and it never is a right one. They simply become the slaves of their own invention. They arrive at an idea about the nature of life and then try to live by it. Their personal standards become their God. Some of them may approximate God's own; others are far from them. How foolish it is for them to persist in their feeble groping when the full light of day could be theirs. It is the responsibility of the children of God to bring them out of their darkness, if they want the light. If they prefer their own inventions, they will be left to them. The hour of crisis will reveal their folly (10:15).

The most common idol before which the world falls down today is materialism. Whether communism or capitalism, the same god is being worshiped. Man works and slaves in order to get for himself all the things that he has made with his own hands. The major difference between communism and capitalism is not what god should be followed but how he should be served. Whether the laborers or private property owners lead in his worship, it is still the great god mammon that is being exalted.

Nehru of India shocked thinking people in America when he said that Russia and the United States possess essentially the same kind of cultures. The first concern of both is the acquisition of things. Spiritual values are secondary. If this is true, our country is in a more serious condition than Russia, for Russia openly states its materialistic philosophy while we delude ourselves into thinking that we honor God. Whereas Communists are openly atheistic, we acknowledge God with our lips but deny him with our lives. It is not that this type of church member is immoral but rather that he is unconcerned. His life is so full of the attractive creations of man's own hands and mind that he does not have time for the eternal truths of God. They can wait until he leaves this good earth. There will be time enough to enjoy spiritual things when material joys are taken away, he thinks. Such a person will wake up in eternity to discover that he has developed no appreciation of spiritual things. Hell is the only place for him, for if he were to go to heaven, he would be very uncomfortable there. The man who finds it difficult to sit through one worship service a week could find no satisfaction in serving and praising God forever. Only those who walk with the living God now will dwell with him in eternity.

II. TRUE WISDOM

1. *Recognizes the Inability of Man to Direct Himself* (8:14-22; 10:23-24)

Jeremiah declared that when God should pour his wrath upon them, the people would see the truth about themselves. When they would drink the "water of gall" (8:14) and hear the snorting of the enemy's horses as the invasion began (8:16), all their pride would be silenced (8:14). Man is at his wisest when he sees himself a wretched sinner in need of the grace of God (8:14), for that is his true condition.

As faithful and devoted as the prophet himself was, he well realized that it was not in his own power to find his way. A crawling infant does not teach himself to walk. He learns from those who already know. Just so a man needs a higher Being to guide his uncertain walk through life. Even Jeremiah needed to be corrected by God when he took a step in the wrong direction. Yet he pleaded with God to temper his judgment with mercy. If God treated him as he deserved, God would utterly destroy him (10:23–24).

2. *Found Only in Knowledge of God* (9:23–24)

There are several attainments in which the natural man is tempted to glory. Those who have superior knowledge are always prone toward letting it affect their ego. Else why do they so often put it on display rather than consider it as an investment by God to be used for the help of other inquiring minds? Knowledge is meant to be used, not to be exhibited.

Other men glory in their strength. "A show of strength" is tempting to individuals as well as nations. The author once was pastor of a church that had enjoyed unprecedented growth. The last Sunday during his pastorate, he asked all those who had joined the church since he came as pastor to come forward. The front of the church was crowded, leaving only a handful of older members in the pews. It was then that Satan entered into the young preacher (who else could it have been?), and he suddenly turned to those in front. "Now let's all vote the others out of the church," he suggested. The startled looks on the faces of all present were not completely gone when the pastor revealed that it was just a joke. It was a joke, yes, but on him. Although in jest, he had yielded to the temptation of a "show of strength."

Others take pride in their riches. Every opportunity is found to display their superior position in society. If the typical American will go to any length to try to impress people with a pretended status, how much more glory it would be actually to have it! He drives a car he cannot afford, lives in a house he can never pay for, throws parties that nearly bankrupt him—all for the approval that may come to him. What a false set of values; how passing a fantasy!

There is only one kind of glorying that is sound: a man's rejoicing that he has found God. He cannot say enough about this wonderful Friend. There are many gods that men follow, but the living God is the one who judges all men. What is so amazing about this great God is that he finds ways to be just, yet loving. In him righteousness and mercy are ideally joined. The Creator rejoices in nothing more than judging men with understanding and equity (9:24). How wonderful it is to know him, for when one stands before God, his Maker, he will understand his inner longings and see that love triumphs over justice. Praise his name!

3. *Perceives the Signs of the Times* (9:12–22; 10:17–22)

It is the rare man who accurately can interpret the meaning of the contemporary scene. Many different meanings can be read into some happenings. Trouble had come upon Judah: "Death is come up into our windows, and is entered into our palaces" (9:21). Why had it happened? Some interpreters believed that it was just the unhappy world situation. Egypt, Assyria, and Babylon were locked in mortal combat, and Israel was caught between them. Others saw in it the purifying of the country. God would take away the dross and leave the pure metal. Those surviving in Jerusalem would be the chosen ones of the Lord. The prophet Jeremiah did not so view the situation. God had shown him the real significance of the events. Only from the divine perspective could the events of earth be seen in their proper light.

"Who is wise enough to see the meaning of this distress?" asked Jeremiah (9:12). The answer came from God, not from Jeremiah's reason: "Because they have forsaken my law which I set before them, and have not obeyed my voice"

(9:13). The day of God's wrath had arrived. He was not so much purifying as he was destroying. There was not even a remnant deserving the name.

Today's world is also a troubled one. What is God about to do in the world? Something momentous is about to happen. What is it to be? Two preachers spoke on successive Wednesday nights in the same church. Afterward one of the members cornered a pastor friend to ask: "Tell me, which of them am I supposed to believe? The first doctor delivered a most convincing sermon. He described the tragic conditions of the world. From this he could only draw one conclusion. We have come to the very last days. Christ is soon to come again and end this troubled age. The small band of the faithful who heard him that night went home in a mood to start settling their earthly affairs.

"Then," he said, "the other good doctor came to speak the next week. He started out the same way as did the other, and we all began to be afraid that the Lord might come before we could get away from the church. Of all places to be when the Lord returned, the church was the last place we wanted to be found, for we had an idea that his wrath might begin right there!

"All of a sudden, however, his message took a different turn. 'It will not be wise to start packing for the other world,' he said, 'for it is always darkest before the dawn. Around the corner is the brightest age the world has ever known.'" The hearer was naturally perplexed. Which speaker was right? Or were they both wrong? Or both right?

Who can properly interpret the meaning of the events of our day? Only the man to whom God reveals himself. Yet numerous are the men who claim that divine word. Which one is correct only the future will tell. Meanwhile we must be careful what we say or believe. Nothing is so unreliable as the wisdom of men or so certain as the purpose of God.

Fortunate indeed are the people who have a true prophet among them. How much more wonderful if they will heed him.

Not only are we perplexed about the divine purpose behind the events of our times, but equally problematical are our own responsibilities. Not only do we need to know what God is doing but also what the Lord will have us do. In the case of the people of Jeremiah's day there was only one course to follow in the prophet's opinion. It was too late to save the city. All the people could do was take whatever came, hoping to survive somehow the blast of God's wrath (10:17-19).

It is to be hoped that the hour is not that late for our country. The presence in it of so many godly people would indicate that there is still time. What God is about to do is still not clear to most of us. Meanwhile, what are we to do? It would appear that we should be busy at what we know to be the work of God. We are to get to the main task, the salvation of a lost world. Not knowing how much time is left, let us use what we have as if it were our last moments.

If we knew that the end was upon us, there should be no difference between the message we would preach and the one we now proclaim. Life is uncertain for every man in the ordinary run of things. Exact information would probably give us a stronger note of urgency, but knowledge of the end should not be necessary for the sounding of the note of alarm. It is evident that man's situation on this globe is desperate, no matter from what direction one views it. Only Christ has the answer, and although he will not always reveal to us all that we would like to know, he will tell us everything that we need to know.

III. THE FOOLISHNESS OF ISRAEL (8:4-7)

Rather than follow the course of wisdom and seek help from God, Jeremiah's people had "slidden back by a perpetual backsliding" (8:5). They continued to go steadily downhill. Usually when a man falls down he will try to get up again; but Israel made no effort to recover from her fall away from God (8:4). When a man leaves home, he usually will return one day. Not so with Israel. In this she showed herself to have less sense than the homing birds (8:7). They know when it is time to return home, but God's people leave and have no desire to return. They rush headlong away from God as a horse rushing into battle, without a glance behind. No one ever stops to take inventory (8:6), to check on the state of his affairs.

Israel was rushing madly after the object of her desires, never asking how far she had gone from home. Serious thoughts might disturb her enjoyment of her sin. Besides, a full awareness of her condition might make it necessary to try to return. She was too busy in sin to be disturbed.

The English words "think" and "thank" are from the same root. If we can get a man to stop long enough to give a few serious thoughts to his soul's condition, we may lead him back to God. Men estranged from God are restless, but they seldom realize the reason for their uneasiness. True wisdom will lead a man to let God take inventory of his life. Only his Maker can properly evaluate his solvency.

FOR STUDY AND DISCUSSION

1. List some similarities between the United States and Russia. What are some differences? Is the United States a Christian nation?
2. In what do you take pride? What does God look upon with pride? Is there a conflict here?
3. What is more difficult, to memorize Scripture passages or to interpret the Scriptures? Does this mean that one should not memorize passages?
4. What are the idols that men worship today? How will each one eventually prove disappointing?

CHAPTER 5 OUTLINE

I. THE REASONS FOR HIS PERSONAL CONFLICTS
1. Inactivity
2. Enforced Loneliness (16:1–21)
3. The Attacks of Those He Loved (11:18 ff.; 18:18–20)
4. Prosperity of the Wicked (12:1–3)
5. The Nature of His Call

II. JEREMIAH'S REACTION TO ADVERSITY
1. Desire to Escape Responsibility (9:1–2)
2. Self-Pity (20:14 ff.)
3. Curses on His Enemies (12:3; 18:21–22)

III. THE DIVINE RESPONSE TO JEREMIAH
1. The Worst Yet to Come (12:5 f.)
2. Jeremiah's Fundamental Problem (15:15 ff.)

IV. THE RESOLVING OF THE INNER CONFLICTS
1. Settled in Prayer
2. The Complaints Cease

5

Jeremiah's Confessions

11:18 to 20:18

THROUGHOUT JEREMIAH 11:18 to 20:18 are to be found extraordinarily frank expressions of Jeremiah's personal struggles. They provide a more intimate picture of his inner life than that of any other person of the Old Testament era. Evidently he bared his soul to Baruch, who in turn preserved for posterity this record of a noble man's spiritual pilgrimage. In these passages it is revealed that the prophet was a man like unto us, yet valiantly pressing toward the light he could see.

The confessions of Jeremiah reveal that he was undergoing tremendous inner conflicts. It seemed that God had no real concern for him (20:7). Life brought him only misery and wretchedness (20:18). God had apparently failed him in his most desperate hour of need (15:18). When he tried to quit preaching, he could not, for the word of God burned like fire in his bones and could not be confined to his own heart (20:9). In other words, he was miserable when he preached, and even more so when he did not. How could he find a solace for his grief?

It will be profitable to examine Jeremiah's confessions, for most people are confronted with similar frustrations. Jeremiah left this record of the torment of his soul that we may not only escape his errors but win his victory. It is most fortunate that he has left behind this stirring record of his inner turmoil, for his trying experiences can help us understand our own.

What caused this crisis in the great prophet's ministry?

I. The Reasons for His Personal Conflicts

1. *Inactivity*

Although Jeremiah was called to preach in 626 B.C. and preached boldly during the next four years (chaps. 1–7), there is no record of his activities after 622 until 609, when he appeared at Josiah's funeral. What was he doing during this interval? At first he was solidly behind Josiah's reformations, even touring the country encouraging the revival (11:1–17). Soon, however, he could see that the change had occurred primarily in the cultic manifestations of piety rather than in heartfelt repentance (3:10). He did not want to interfere with Josiah's efforts, for he believed in them, yet he could see that the people were not genuine enough in their response. Perhaps even yet the reform would soon reach deeper. At any length, the leadership of the godly king had clearly given Jerusalem a reprieve. The situation was no longer desperate, as it was when the prophet first was called. It appeared certain that it would one day reach that stage again, but meanwhile Jeremiah waited, watched, hoped, and had little to say.

With the coming of Jehoiakim to the throne, the situation deteriorated rapidly. The time had come to reiterate the words of doom. Being seventeen years older than when he was called, Jeremiah had lost some of his youthful recklessness. The doors were rusty on their hinges, and much of the initial fire had burned low.

Churches, after a period of great activity, are tempted to settle back for a rest. Once this has happened, it takes a miracle to get them moving again. *Rigor mortis* begins before it is suspected. Men work hard all their lives in order to enjoy the years of retirement; yet as soon as the time arrives and they settle down for a well-earned rest, their health starts to trouble them for the first time. Often they would live longer if, freed from some of the ordinary tensions, they continued an active and useful life.

After thirteen years of comparative inactivity as a prophet, Jeremiah was having trouble shifting into high gear! Man is not yet equipped with automatic drive. He must keep in practice.

2. Enforced Loneliness (16:1–21)

There are some people who enjoy being alone, but Jeremiah was not that kind of person. He longed for nothing more than to spend pleasant hours in good company (9:2). Perhaps a certain dark-eyed damsel had already caught his eye. None of this was for him, however. It would not be right for him to marry and bring children into such an evil time (16:2). They would only see grief and calamity (16:3–4). God even forbade his attending the outstanding social events of his community, funerals and weddings. In the Orient these occasions were not just times to show grief or joy, but a rare opportunity for friends to congregate. He was not to attend funerals because it was senseless to grieve over the death of a departed loved one, since he was so much more fortunate than those who were left behind. The living were the ones over whom to weep since such dire tragedy lay ahead for all (16:5–6).

Neither was he to frequent weddings. It would not be fitting to participate in such merriment, since nothing but disaster lay ahead for the devoted couples (16:9). It would be inappropriate for him to attend festive occasions of any sort, for the odor of death was hanging about them all (16:8).

In addition to the prohibitions placed upon him by God, as Jeremiah faithfully proclaimed his message the people began to ostracize him. It is one thing to separate yourself from your community by choice and quite another to discover that you would not be wanted if you chose to appear. The lonely soul always validates the original observations of the Creator himself, "It is not good that the man should be alone" (Gen. 2:18).

3. *The Attacks of Those He Loved* (11:18 ff; 18:18–20)

Jeremiah's friends did not stop with avoiding him, however. They began to persecute him, sometimes with that cruelest of weapons, their tongues (18:18), but just as often with determined efforts to destroy him bodily (11:21). What made it doubly difficult was the fact that these were those whom he loved, whom he had counted upon as friends if trouble came. Those who first sought his life were either his boyhood friends from his home town (11:21) or the very people for whom he had earnestly pleaded before God (18:20), trying to persuade God to spare them.

An eminent administrator once told his listeners that it is a well-established pattern that the people who receive most of the executive's attention will be the ones who will eventually work for his downfall. It was David's intimate friend Ahithophel who betrayed him to Absalom; Judas was traitor to Jesus; it took Brutus to destroy Caesar. Whether it is Caesar, Jeremiah, you, or I, there is no dismay so great as that occasioned by the point of the assassin's knife in the hand of one thought to be a friend. To be destroyed by one's enemies is not too surprising, but we are never prepared for betrayal. It was in this respect that Jesus most vividly displayed his wisdom, for he was not caught by surprise. Yet anticipation did not take the sting out of it.

4. *Prosperity of the Wicked* (12:1–3)

It was difficult enough for Jeremiah to face the rejection of those he loved and the adversity that was its consequence. His burden became unbearable, however, when he noticed that, on the contrary, wicked men were prospering all the more. Was God truly in command in his world? Why did he plant them so firmly that they grew and multiplied? If the lot of the righteous is difficult, the way of the transgressor should be harder. Yet the opposite is too often true. As the good man falls, the wicked ascends to power: "Truth for ever on the scaffold, wrong for ever on the throne." This was Job's problem, the tortured question of the afflicted psalmist, and the honest inquiry of every saint sorely beset.

Why is it that some of the best people suffer the most while the worst often live out their days in honor? Admittedly this insoluble question bursts out as naturally from the anguished soul as a rocket from its launching pad. It is not the smug inquiry of the uncommitted cynic, but the desperate plea of a man who will trust God whether he gets the answer or not (12:1). He will carry his load whether or no, but it will make it easier if he knows why. Until that time comes, he reserves the right to complain, even as he wearily but steadily plods on.

5. *The Nature of His Call*

It was inevitable that Jeremiah would have serious personal problems, for his call to prophesy reveals a man who was at war within himself. The man who proceeds to serve God because it is his duty but with an inner recoiling from such a path always finds rough sailing ahead. Of course it is better to follow God from a sense of duty than not to follow him at all, but such an attitude is a poor substitute. Until God's will for us has become our own personal desire, the struggle for supremacy within us will continue.

The man who proclaims that he is in the ministry not because in it he finds fulfillment but because God has drafted him against his will, in effectiveness will fall far short of the man who gives himself to preaching because there is nothing else he prefers before it. This is not to depreciate those who have been drafted into the ministry, for some of our best men have had this type of call. Eventually, however, these noble men have come to see that God was wiser than they, and they gladly give themselves to the task from which they once shrank. Jeremiah started his career of prophesying because it was commanded of God. He would have preferred another walk of life. Whenever anything went wrong, therefore, he would be all the more convinced that God had laid his hand on the wrong man. Such an inner conflict was not likely to contribute toward the prophet's peace of mind in times of adversity. In fact, it resulted in a soul at war with itself.

II. JEREMIAH'S REACTION TO ADVERSITY

When his contemporaries began to reject and persecute him, Jeremiah responded in the three ways that usually characterize the behavior of a man who is so treated.

1. *Desire to Escape Responsibility* (9:1-2)

The prophet's first desire was to get away from it all. What was to be gained by preaching to such unresponsive people, by sleepless nights of worry over their coming doom? His was not a desire to become a hermit, for he did not want to get away from people. Jeremiah was a man who loved others and liked to be with them. Accordingly his desire was not to be alone but rather to be rid of any responsibility for the future welfare of others. If he could just run an inn in the wilderness! Then he could be with people constantly, yet not be responsible for them except for the one night they stayed with him. They could talk and laugh, and then he could even preach to them a while. Tomorrow, however, they would go on their way, and he could be rid of any worry over how they had responded to his words. A new group would come in, and he could face the challenge of a fresh opportunity to witness. But to preach to the same old unresponsive crowd, this was more than one could endure. Oh, to be able to throw off the burden!

For the dedicated man there is no such relief possible. Where can God go? To some remote corner of the universe to create a new world while this one goes to ruin? Of course not! Nor can a dedicated man afford to run away. Many a man leaves a difficult situation only to turn his back upon greatness. The time for a minister to leave, if it is in his control, is when he has succeeded, not after failure. We emphasize, of course, if it is in his control. If one is in a situation in which it is not only apparent that he has failed, but will continue to do so, while someone else could make a better contribution, the better decision would be to admit defeat and move on to a situation where he could profit from past mistakes. The author has played in too many athletic games to advise anyone to keep on playing after the game-ending whistle has been blown.

The reason why Jeremiah was forced to continue even with the certain prospect of failure was the fact that anyone else would also have failed. If there had to be a failure, why should he not be the one? Christians have too readily today allowed the success psychology of a worldly society to determine their actions. They too often think that unless they win the recognition of their contemporaries they have fallen short. Yet the very meaning of the cross is that its way leads to rejection by men but exaltation by God. Fortunate indeed is the man who has been chosen by God to fight a losing battle, for it is only then that he truly walks with God, who also has experienced the necessity of losing before he can win (12:7–17).

Jeremiah, like any troubled soul, longed to get away from responsibility. However, the dedicated man that he was, he never left his post of duty. Yet you cannot keep a man from dreaming! Little children have been taught to sing the chorus:

> I've been working for the Lord a long, long time
> and I ain't got weary yet.

However, this little poem is disturbing, for the innocent little folks are being taught a false view of life. Anyone who has been working for the Lord a long, long time has often grown weary and has been tempted to quit. Yet at the very moment one thinks he has made his last step, God will give strength to take another. As long as the faithful servant can take another step, he will never leave the service of his master.

2. Self-Pity (20:14 ff.)

When things go wrong, one of the most certain reactions is to feel sorry for oneself. The author remembers lines from a song of his boyhood that often have expressed his saddest thoughts:

> Nobody loves me, everybody hates me
> I'm going to the garden and eat worms.

Adversity invariably leads to our feeling sorry for ourselves as the most unfortunate of all people. Jeremiah was no different. His lowest moment came just after he had suffered the indignities of the public stocks. Helpless before the insults of his enemies, Jeremiah had been cursed and spit upon all day. No wonder he was discouraged. Not only did he want no one to remember his birthday but he pronounced a curse upon it for being of all days the most unfortunate (20:14). Indeed he felt called upon to curse the man who informed his father of his birth. Such sad news should have been suppressed, not broadcast! The very idea of anyone's thinking that the world had been blessed by such an event—a child born to suffering and despair, not only for himself but for all those he loved! Because that man did not slay him at birth, he asked God to destroy him as he did Sodom and Gomorrah. A crime indeed it was to permit such a monstrosity to live! Of course, all of this is poetry, and it is not to be taken literally. By the use of exaggeration the prophet depreciated loudly the worthwhileness of his existence. Jeremiah even felt that it would have been better had he been stillborn. Far better even that his mother continue to carry her unborn child forever than to give birth to such an accursed child! All that he was due to experience was pain, sorrow, and shame, until he eventually wasted away. Why be born into that kind of existence?

This passage is reminiscent of the third chapter of Job, where that patriarch was in a similar mood. It also leads one to recall the discouragement of Elijah during his flight from the wrath of Jezebel. All men are subject to such moments. They are the marks of a true humanity. They become unhealthy when they are prolonged or occur too frequently. They come to us in order to give us a springboard from which to rise to a better view of the horizon. They are never meant to be our abiding place. Once such moods come, they must be quickly dispelled by faith.

It is here that Jeremiah was handicapped by not having a good wife. How often have men of God faced discouragement and despair only to be sent on their way encouraged by the confidence of a faithful companion. No man ever finds life senseless and futile who knows the love of a devoted wife. All the more credit to Jeremiah that he survived his ordeal alone. He was made of sterner stuff than some of us.

3. *Curses on His Enemies* (12:3; 18:21-22)

The typical Old Testament saint hated his enemies with all the intensity with which he hated sin itself. Jeremiah was no exception. He called upon the Lord to select them for slaughter the way the shepherd separates the sheep for market (12:3). He prayed that the children of his tormentors be delivered up to famine and sword and that their wives be bereaved both of husbands and sons (18:21-22). Fiercely he asked that in their time of trouble their god would neither hear their prayer nor forgive their iniquity.

How was it possible that a man so close to God could have such feelings as these? There are several matters to be considered. First, even after Christ has come to reveal the necessity of love, we Christians still have difficulty loving one another. No wonder the Hebrews had problems. It is natural for a hurt animal to strike back, and our lower natures keep clamoring for supremacy. Psalms 137 and 109 clearly reveal that the best of Old Testament worshipers felt it appropriate to hate their enemies. Again, the devoted Hebrews identified themselves with the cause of God. To attack them was identical with an offense against deity. Men were to be cursed not so much because they were personal enemies but because of their stand against the word of God. They found it impossible to hate sin but love the sinner. Such spiritual gymnastics are still not easy to perfect.

Further, Jeremiah's offer of love had been spurned (18:20). The prophet had earnestly prayed for these people and tried to help them. They had returned evil for good. There is no hurt so deep as the wound resulting from rejected love. As a mother bear defends her endangered cubs, a man fights against those who would destroy his love. To desecrate his love is the cruelest blow of all. Here, more than anywhere else, he finds it difficult to be sweet tempered.

Also it is evident that the Old Testament saint's attitude was colored by his thinking about the after-life. Although some of the passages indicate a confidence in a positive life with God after death (Gen. 5:24; Dan. 12:2), most of the Old Testament is quite pessimistic about such a hope (Psalm 39:13; Isa. 38:18). Jeremiah gives little evidence of having a strong faith in life after death. The only passage in the book that gives any other indication is Jeremiah 17:13, where the Lord says that "they that depart from me shall be written in the earth." If the wicked are written in the earth, then the righteous must be written in heaven on the rolls of eternity. Yet this implication can only be inferred here; it is not clearly proclaimed.

The average Hebrew writer believed that God rewarded a man in this life, whether for good or for evil. He did not have our comfort—that the wicked will get his due reward in eternity. If he did not receive it here and now, then the justice of God had failed. When Jeremiah prayed for God to destroy the wicked, he was pleading that justice should be done. If it did not happen before the eyes of the living, the universe was no longer attuned to the righteous ways of the Lord.

The only passage in the Old Testament that approximates the Christian attitude of love for one's enemies is in Job 31:29–30. Here Job said that to curse one's enemy is a sin and denied that it had brought him any delight to see any of his enemies fall. It is even more striking that he said this after he had come to a triumphant faith in life after death (Job 19:23–27). There is nothing like the doctrine of heaven to ease one's concern over the insolence of the wicked. Without this assurance one could hardly be disposed toward letting things take their natural course.

Finally, it is apparent that Jeremiah himself never laid unfriendly hands upon any man. The prophet did not allow himself to raise the sword against another, although that one might give him provocation. His tongue was his sword. The rest he left up to God. To take the law of God into our own hands is one thing. To pray for God to begin his work of wrath is quite another, for only as his wrath is in action can his love eventually triumph.

Although Jeremiah's curses upon his enemies cannot be defended in the light of the attitude taught us by Jesus, yet neither can we condemn him. Those who are without sin will have to cast the first stone. We will have a right to criticize him only when we are as true to our light as he was to his.

III. THE DIVINE RESPONSE TO JEREMIAH

It is instructive to examine the manner in which God dealt with the prophet's complaints. He would not permit Jeremiah to put him on the defensive in respect to his handling of the prophet's ministry in the affairs of the world. Rather he set Jeremiah back upon his heels in dismay.

1. *The Worst Yet to Come* (12:5 f.)

God informed Jeremiah that this was no time for him to become discouraged, for the long haul was yet ahead. He had just been running with the footmen. If he let them weary him, he would never be able to keep up when the time came to race with the horses.

The latter part of verse 5 admits of two interpretations, depending upon how one relates the "land of peace" with the "swelling of Jordan." Some interpreters say that the contrast is between a peaceful season along the Jordan and the time of its flooding. Others say that the comparison is between the peaceful Jordan valley and the bush jungle found along its banks, where lions and other wild animals often lurked. The word translated "swelling" can mean pride. The jungle of the Jordan could be referred to here as its proudest possession. The "pride of the Jordan" accordingly would be the "jungle of the Jordan." Whatever sense one gives to the passage, however, the same general meaning emerges. If Jeremiah became disheartened in peaceful times, how would he ever endure the future stresses of life? God was saying to the prophet, "Cheer up, Jeremiah. The worst is yet to come."

There is not too much comfort in such counsel, but it does give fair warning to the man of God. He must not let down his guard, for the good fight of faith is never done. Each skirmish today prepares for the tougher engagement tomorrow. As practice prepares a team for the crucial game, the frustrations of today ready the players for the crises yet to come. How we run today likely will determine the outcome tomorrow. If the worst is yet to come, and it usually is, it is a great mistake to become fainthearted in the present crisis. For the fainthearted there can be no future.

The author's family hiked the trail down into the Grand Canyon and to the Colorado River, a total of eight miles. A short way back they became weary and footsore but dared not stop for long. They still had six miles to go, and these were all straight up! There was little comfort in this knowledge, but nevertheless it kept them from dallying until it was impossible to get out. Thus it was with Jeremiah.

2. *Jeremiah's Fundamental Problem* (15:15 ff.)

It is in this passage that Jeremiah betrayed the basic reason for all his discouragement. In four verses (15:15-18) he used the first person (I, me, my) sixteen times! His fundamental problem was that he was too concerned about what he himself must endure. Rather than concentrate upon the mission that was his, and the desperate plight of Judah, he was crying his heart out over his own personal frustrations. The true minister of God must not concern himself with his personal future, but losing himself, devote his life to his calling. Jeremiah had managed to get his perspective out of focus.

The Lord called his attention to this dangerous situation (15:19). The verb *shuv*, translated "return," is the usual verb that means repent. The man who truly repents "turns" from his evil ways and back to God. Thus he "returns" to God. The verb is also commonly used in the sense of "turn" without reference to repentance. Thus it emphasizes the necessity of changing one's behavior before he can be reconciled to God.

Thus, in effect, God said to Jeremiah, "If you change your ways, I will restore you, and you can be my prophet [stand before me]."

Jeremiah was in danger of losing his place in the service of God. Unless he got his mind off himself and his own frustration, he was finished as a mouthpiece for God. He must learn to distinguish between the precious and the common (vile) or he could not continue to serve (15:20). Anyone can talk like Jeremiah had been talking. It is quite common to hear men complaining because life has not treated them according to their liking. Jeremiah must rise above this and start proclaiming the precious truths of God rather than bemoan the adverse treatment he had received.

If a man has lost himself in the purposes of God, he will not be overly sensitive to personal frustration. His first concern will be for the cause he represents. Whatever heartbreak arises will be due to the rejection of the truth he proclaims rather than to mistreatment from his fellows. Personal fulfilment is to be found in losing oneself in the will of God. Until one does this he cannot truly be God's spokesman. Rather he is more likely to speak only for himself, his own unhappiness blinding him to the impulses that come from above. Eventually he becomes more sensitive to what men are saying than to what God speaks, more responsive to their insults than to the wooings of the Eternal.

IV. The Resolving of the Inner Conflicts

It is gratifying that the personal tensions that characterized Jeremiah's earlier ministry were resolved in his later years. The solution was reached in the only way possible to faltering man.

1. Settled in Prayer

Although Jeremiah's complaints were numerous and vociferous, it is remarkable that these were always directed at

God, not to man. Whatever problems were his, he did not take them to his neighbor but to his God. Unlike Job he did not criticize to his companions the injustice of God, but always directed his words to the one who had put him in the path he had been forced to follow. In other words, his complaints were prayers.

To Jeremiah prayer was not just petition or thanksgiving but was marked by an intimate sharing of his secret soul. Whatever his tensions, he would bring them before God. Always he would discover that the Lord was a sympathetic listener, although frequently he was instructed to change his attitude, which was what he needed to hear. Although God expected him to bring his doubts to him, he nevertheless would never be satisfied until the questionings were resolved.

In this interplay of conversation between God and prophet, real insight is given into the nature of prophetic inspiration. The man of God was not merely a stenographer who copied down what was dictated to him. He was a dedicated servant whose every thought was afire with the struggle for divine light upon the chaos of human affairs. God communicated his truth because the prophet could not be satisfied until the divine manna fell on his soul.

The intimate experiences of Jeremiah had a profound influence upon the writers of the psalms. A direct relationship is obvious between Jeremiah 17:5–8 and Psalm 1. Who fails to be reminded of Jeremiah when he hears the psalmist crying out to God of injustice and unmerited persecution and asking for the wrath of God upon Israel's enemies? Did these psalms influence Jeremiah or did the words of the prophet provide the atmosphere for them? Perhaps both are true, but the indebtedness is heavier on the part of the Psalter.[1]

However, it is the concept of the Servant of the Lord that

---

[1] Cf. Robert Furman Kenney, "Jeremiah's Distinctive Contribution to Hebrew Psalmody." Unpublished doctoral thesis, Southern Baptist Theological Seminary, 1952.

most clearly reflects the experiences of Jeremiah. He, too, has been chosen before birth (Isa. 49:1–2), persecuted by his hearers (50:6), and rejected (53:1–6). Yet these sufferings will be redemptive, just as were those of Jeremiah. The difference will be in the task to be accomplished, and the nature of the person who does it.

Out of his sufferings Jeremiah gave his people a faith to live by during the dark days of the exile, while the Suffering Servant through his sacrifice will solve for his people not only the problem of doubt but sin itself, of which doubt is only a symptom. The heartbreak and sacrifice of Jeremiah became the basis of the understanding of the ultimate purpose of God for man.

2. *The Complaints Cease*

The confessions of Jeremiah all belong to the Jehoiakim period of the prophet's life. After chapter 20, the complaints abruptly cease. Upon his knees the perplexed man of God had found his inner peace. Whatever might come, he would be able to face it with assurance in the providence of God. Having outrun the horsemen, he was ready for the horses!

This latter state of mind resembles the description in Isaiah 53:7 as the Servant of the Lord is characterized: "He was oppressed, and he was afflicted, yet he opened not his mouth: he is brought as a lamb to the slaughter, and as a sheep before her shearers is dumb, so he openeth not his mouth." Nothing could be farther from Jeremiah's earlier attitude than this passage. Yet it vividly portrays what he had finally learned to do. What Jeremiah had to achieve in the furnace of affliction, the future Redeemer would instinctively know. Who can deny that Jeremiah's experiences somehow clarified for the Saviour himself the significance of his ultimate sacrifice? We are all aware of the fact that the Old Testament was inspired in order to prepare the world for the Christ. Yet we do not always realize that since it was the only Bible that Jesus possessed as a lad, it also served to prepare the Christ for the world. It inevitably revealed to him the path he must travel.

FOR STUDY AND DISCUSSION

1. What light do the confessions of Jeremiah throw upon the true nature of prayer? Upon prophetic inspiration?
2. What are some of your own responsibilities? How do you react to them?
3. Using a concordance, investigate the two principal Hebrew views concerning the afterlife. Which is more prominent in the earlier books of the Old Testament? Why?
4. Does Isaiah 40–55 precede or follow Jeremiah in time of writing?[2] What difference does it make in their interpretation?

---

[2] Cf. Clyde T. Francisco, *Introducing the Old Testament* (Nashville: Broadman Press, 1950), pp. 116–118.

CHAPTER 6 OUTLINE

I. THE DECEITFULNESS OF THE HEART (17:9–10)
  1. Likened to Jacob
  2. Its Incomparable Deceitfulness

II. THE HEART INCURABLY AFFLICTED
  1. The Blinding Nature of Sin (13:22; 16:10)
  2. The Enslaving Power of Sin (13:23)
  3. Sin unto Death (17:9)

III. THE CURE OF THE HEART
  1. Only God Can Diagnose (17:9–10)
  2. Balm from Gilead (8:18 to 9:1)

IV. THE FREEDOM OF THE HEART (18:1 to 19:15)
  1. Free Will and Divine Sovereignty
  2. The Conditional Nature of Prophecy

6

The Depravity of the Heart

13:1 to 19:15

IN THE BOOK OF JEREMIAH are to be found the clearest teachings concerning human depravity in the Old Testament. Chapters 1–3 of Genesis clearly teach that man was originally created in the image of God. Then sin entered into the Garden and the image became marred although still present (Gen. 5:3). Jeremiah adds to this picture the convictions born of his own experience. It is not necessary to go to the Bible to know that man is depraved. One only has to look deep into his own heart. If any man ever walked closely with God, Jeremiah did. His call experience bears no mark of any consciousness of sin. The living presence of God brought no dismay to the young Hebrew. No one ever wanted to do the will of God more than Jeremiah. He was consumed by a desire to represent God to his nation. Yet in spite of his good intentions and genuine love, Jeremiah soon discovered that his own heart was betraying him. What he longed to do for God his own nature rebelled against. If a sincere and dedicated believer had trouble with himself, how much more would this characterize others.

I. THE DECEITFULNESS OF THE HEART (17:9–10)

The Hebrews used the term "heart" in quite a different way from our own use. Whereas to us the heart is either the organ that pumps blood or the center of the emotional life, to the ancients it was all this and more! All the functions of the inner man were attributed to it. The Assyrian king Sennacherib was said to think with his heart as well as to use it as the source of his will (Isa. 10:7). The inner voice of the heart is called the conscience. The Hebrews would simply call it the heart.

1. *Likened to Jacob*

In Jeremiah 17:9 the prophet described the heart as deceitful. This word is from the same root as the proper noun "Jacob," which means a deceiver or trickster. Even as Jacob tricked his brother Esau and fooled his father Isaac, just so every man's heart will deceive him. Jeremiah was giving the lie to the common proverb, "Let your conscience be your guide." "Your heart will bear constant watching," he claimed, "for it is likely to fool you." How right he was.

2. *Its Incomparable Deceitfulness*

Not only is the heart a deceiver, the prophet pointed out, but it is the worst of all deceitful things. There are many things and people that are likely to fool a man, but his own heart is the worst of all. His own inner voice is the most dangerous enemy he has.

The author once thought that although God could protect him from every danger as long as he trusted him, there was no reason why he could not choose to leave God of his own accord. Now he realizes that if God does not protect him from himself he is not under his care at all, for he is left exposed before his most treacherous enemy, his own deceitful heart. Of all things the heart is the most misleading.

II. THE HEART INCURABLY AFFLICTED

The trouble with the heart is that it is afflicted with a dread disease that has three direct consequences.

1. *The Blinding Nature of Sin* (13:22; 16:10)

The disease of the heart is all the more serious because the afflicted person does not know he is ill. The affliction gives no warning of its presence; the victim is not aware of the danger. Israel could see no reason why God was so concerned about her. Nothing was wrong so far as she could see (13:22). If iniquity was within her heart, she had not detected it (16:10). There was not the slightest quiver of conscience to warn of imminent catastrophe. All was well in the heart so far as the victim could tell.

It is alarming to realize that one can go all through his life feeling quite certain that he is heading for heaven, when hell is his real destination. A man must keep constant vigil lest he be lulled into the sleep of death by the betrayal of his own heart.

2. *The Enslaving Power of Sin* (13:23)

This passage is often described as teaching the power of sinful habit. This it does teach, but it says more than this. Just as the Ethiopian cannot change his dark skin or the leopard his spots, even so a sinful man cannot change his own disposition to sin. A harmful habit a man can conquer by a supreme effort of will. When a man goes too far in sin and becomes accustomed to it, a condition results that affects the will itself. The color of the Ethiopian's skin or the spots of the leopard are not habit; they characterize their basic nature. Not that they want to change it, however. What leopard would want to change his spots? Lions' coats look dull to him! The man who continues to sin so weakens his will that he is incapable of willing a change in his behavior.

Neither can outward reform change his inner motivation. The alcoholic may quit his drinking but yet not be able to change the character that caused him to be one in the first place. Providing education and better housing conditions for the underprivileged makes life more pleasant for them, but it does not guarantee marital bliss or parental faithfulness. Once man's sinful disposition has established its sway, there is no way that a man can regain his freedom. He is hopelessly entangled. If he could change into an upright person, the leopard would change its spots and the Ethiopian become fair-skinned.

3. *Sin unto Death* (17:9)

The disease of the will is a fatal one. The phrase translated "desperately wicked" literally means mortally ill. The sickness is so severe that unless something is done immediately, death will result. In other words, all men have heart trouble in a spiritual sense. Heart disease is today's number one physical killer in America, but it has always afflicted the soul. The prophet was not saying that some men have this disease while others do not. When he used the expression "the heart," it was equivalent to saying "every heart." Not only is every heart a Jacob and the most deceitful voice a man hears, but the malady with which it is afflicted is a fatal one.

The sinning soul will die, not just as a consequence of an act of God but because of the nature of the disease. It is incurable in its very nature; death is its invariable result. The disease is incipient in the child, who is not held responsible for a nature he did not will. However, as soon as he becomes morally responsible, he loses the battle with temptation and becomes a sinner himself. Jeremiah did not try to explain how this happens; he only knew that it had occurred in his own experience and in the people whom he knew. The sinner is lost not because God arbitrarily sends a helpless man to hell but because the sin that afflicts all men makes fellowship with God impossible. Its very nature corrupts all men and leaves them outside the will of God. Modern theories or explanations are at the most but feeble attempts to rationalize a fact of experience. All men are sinners, regardless of how it comes about, and as sinners they are doomed to die.

III. The Cure of the Heart

Is there any hope for man? Can anything be done for his wretched condition? The prophet is convinced that there is a way out.

1. *Only God Can Diagnose* (17:9–10)

Since man's own conscience will not tell him the truth about himself, he must look elsewhere for an accurate evaluation. Other men cannot give him a reliable analysis, for they have the same kind of heart as his own. Only God can see clearly into the inner recesses of the heart. He alone can accurately test the true source of our desires. The word translated "reins" literally means kidneys, which were regarded as the center of the emotional life, thus controlling (as with reins) a man's behavior. Why do we behave the way we do? Only God can tell us. We would do well to listen to him, for one day we will be judged upon the basis of what he knows about us, rather than our own opinion of ourselves.

There is no way that a man can know the true condition of his heart unless he listens to what God has to say. This is the primary purpose of the Bible. As we hear God speaking there, we are made aware of our true condition. We will not be judged upon the basis of our personal views or the customs of our day or region. Rather, the judgment will be based upon what God has already revealed to us in his Word. We would do well, therefore, to let him show us where we stand today.

2. *Balm from Gilead* (8:18 to 9:1)

Although this passage is found in the section on wisdom, it is especially enlightening at this point, and could well belong chronologically to the Jehoiakim period. The prophet saw Israel under the heel of a cruel conqueror. Time was running out for the condemned nation. Both the time of harvest and the summer had passed, but no crops had been reaped. (The regular season for harvest in Palestine is April–June.) It is in late summer (September) that the final fruits are gathered. There was little chance now for the nation.

Why had this happened? Was it because there was no balm in Gilead, no physician there? Some expositors insist that the answer is no.

> Did you ever feel the pathos of his piercing question—"Is there no balm in Gilead? Is there no physician there?" Gilead was a region which lay on the prophet's eastern horizon. It was over Gilead that the sun rose every morning to illumine little Anathoth and big Jerusalem. It was the land which symbolized hope. In Gilead grew the herbs and trees and flowers from which balsams were made to supply the physicians of that Eastern world. Is there no balm even in Gilead? Is there no physician, no prophet, no priest, no healer, no teacher who can cure a sick heart? And the answer is "No."[1]

Although the answer to Jefferson's question is obviously no, it is apparent that his question and Jeremiah's are not the same. Jeremiah 8:22b requires a positive answer to the prophet's question.

"Is there no balm in Gilead; is there no physician there?" Jeremiah inquired.

"Of course," the people replied, "Gilead is plentiful in medicines, and many are the physicians who are trained there."

"If that is so," answered the prophet, "why are you still sick?"

There could be but one reason. They would not send for the doctor; they would not use the balm. No prophet or priest could heal them, but God had been available all the time. Both the physician and the medicine had been available. Perhaps now it was too late, but there had been a whole

---

[1] Charles E. Jefferson, *Cardinal Ideas of Jeremiah* (New York: The Macmillan Company, 1928), p. 141.

season when they could have been saved. Even now, so late in the year, something might be done if they would call for the physician. Had it been too late for God to heal, Jeremiah would have had no cause for preaching. He did not preach to condemn but to save. As long as there is a prophet, it is never too late to pray: "Heal me, O Lord, and I shall be healed; save me, and I shall be saved" (17:14).

However, if the people continued to try to summon their own physician and use their own balm, there was no hope. It was already too late. The most pessimistic passage in Jeremiah is 14:1 to 15:9. Here a dialogue ensued between Jeremiah and God. A drought had come upon the land, and the prophet, speaking for the people, prayed for divine help (14:1–9). The Lord replied that he could do nothing for them until they changed their ways. It would do no good to pray for them as long as they refused to repent (14:10–12). Jeremiah objected that their prophets had misled the people into a false confidence (14:13) and were really the ones to blame. To this God replied that both prophets and people would be judged—the prophets for preaching falsehood and the people for believing it (14:14–18). "Surely," the people replied, "you will not deny your own people. We have faith to believe that you will help us, and we know that no other god can" (14:19 ff.). God was not impressed by their flattery. Faith without works is useless. No amount of intercession can save a nation or an individual that will not change his ways (15:1–9). God was weary with repenting (15:6), tired of having mercy upon an unresponsive people.

All this is said, however, in light of Israel's refusal to turn from its wicked ways. If the people would but change, there might yet be time. This is what every true man of God hopes in his heart. Even as he preaches inevitable wrath, he hopes against hope for repentance and possible pardon for his people. Although the summer is ended, perhaps a few pieces of fruit or a few grains of wheat may yet be saved.

This message of Jeremiah is a moving commentary upon the conditions that mark our country today. Time is rapidly running out on us, the harvest is already past, the summer about ended. Is there no answer to our problems? Of course there is. The Great Physician, Jesus Christ, has the answer. The reason why we are a sick country is because we will not ask his counsel or accept his prescriptions for our ills. Unless America repents of its materialism and immorality, our wounds will have no healing. If we will repent it may not yet be too late.

IV. THE FREEDOM OF THE HEART (18:1 to 19:15)

In a real sense, the will of man is not free. Before he comes to God he is the slave of sin. Afterward he is the servant of God. Yet he must be free to choose his master. It is possible for him either to yield to God or to resist him. To this extent man's heart decides its own destiny.

1. Free Will and Divine Sovereignty

There is no more intricate problem in Christian theology than the relationship between the sovereignty of God and man's free will. There are many explanations offered, but the significant fact is that both are true. God is the absolute ruler of the universe. Yet man is free to decide his own direction.

As Jeremiah watched a potter at work on his wheel, he was given divine insight into the ways of God with men, whether individuals or nations. His emphasis in this passage is obviously upon God's use of nations (18:5-10), yet one is not doing violence to its meaning if he notices the application to individuals as well.

(1) *The potter had a purpose.*—First Jeremiah noticed that the potter had a purpose for the clay (18:3). Before he began his work, in his mind's eye was a picture of the completed vessel. Just so, God works with man. Before man's life

(or a nation's) begins, God has a plan for each one, even as he had for Jeremiah and Israel. And it is a good purpose. No good potter would design a poor vessel. A man need not fear the will of God for his life or shrink from it. Nothing better could happen to him.

(2) *The clay was marred in the potter's hand* (18:4).— This marring of the clay was not due to the artisan's inefficiency, of course, but to some stubborn spot in the clay. What a tragic truth. Although God has the highest good in mind for every life, that life can become marred. Man can resist the will of God. Such a man will never find happiness, but he can say no to God. Some people have the strange idea that everything that happens is the will of God. Of course, God permits everything that occurs, but what happens is not always his active will. Jesus taught us to pray: "Thy kingdom come. Thy will be done in earth, as it is in heaven" (Matt. 6:10). There would be no point in our praying that God's will should be done on earth if it is already being done. Some years ago a man came home drunk at night and knocked his young baby out of bed. The child died from the injuries. When the neighbors heard about it, one of them said, "That was a terrible thing that happened, but it was the will of God, and God's will be done." Is it the will of God that drunken men should destroy their children? That men should go to hell? That people should hate one another? So much of what goes on in this world is not the way God plans it. The clay is always becoming marred in the potter's hand.

(3) *The potter made another vessel* (18:4).—Man can resist the will of God, but God does not immediately destroy him. He works with the stubborn spot until he gets it out. Then he forms another vessel. It may not be the same one that he first planned but it will be a useful one. There is only one thing that keeps a man from being useful to God: the stubbornness of his own heart. Whenever a man will yield

himself to God, the divine potter will reshape his life. Perhaps he can never be what he could have been at first but he can find his place of service.

(4) *Sometimes it is too late for the clay to be molded.*— In chapter 19, Jeremiah took a potter's vessel that had already been baked in the oven and led the elders to the city dump. There he held the vessel up for their inspection and cast it upon the rocks. Hardened in the oven, it could not be reshaped again. Broken on the rocks it could not be refashioned (19:11). There comes a time when it is too late for the clay to be molded. When a heart turns to stone, there is nothing left to do but abandon it. While the clay is still pliable one must yield. One day it may be too late, for the sovereign God will eventually realize his purpose and those who resist it will be destroyed.

2. *The Conditional Nature of Prophecy*

Although the individual implications are obvious in these chapters, yet these were not Jeremiah's immediate concern. The primary lesson that Jeremiah learned from the potter concerned God's response to nations. His actions are not so much conditioned by prophetic promises as by the moral behavior of the nations involved. Just as the clay must yield to the potter's touch in order for the vessel to be made, so nations must surrender to God's purposes. Just because God has expressed through one of his prophets a great ideal for Israel, that does not necessarily mean it will be achieved. The clay may become marred in the potter's hand (18:9–10).

There are some expositors who insist that if a promise is made to Israel in the Old Testament, it will one day come to pass literally. Yet Jeremiah makes it quite plain that the opposite is true. All prophecies are morally conditioned, whether it is clearly stated or not. God may speak through a prophet that he intends to bless Israel, but if that nation does evil in his sight, it will lose its right to the promises. These

same blessings will one day come to a people who are obedi-
ent to God. The promise is fulfilled, but only to those who
meet God's original intention.

Likewise it is true that if a prophecy contains a curse upon
a nation, God will not honor it if the nation concerned repents of its sins and turns to God (18:7–8). This is what is
involved in the book of Jonah. The primary reason why
Jonah did not want to go to Nineveh was that he would be
embarrassed as a prophet. He would predict its destruction,
and the people would repent. Then God would have mercy
upon them and spare the city. Thus Jonah's prediction would
not happen. This was exactly how matters proceeded when
Jonah belatedly arrived in Nineveh. God condemned the
prophet for being more concerned about himself than he was
for the lives of the people of Nineveh. Jeremiah underscored
a significant fact about God. He is more concerned about the
moral and ethical responses of people than the literal fulfilment of a promise. It is better that a prophet be embarrassed
than that a repentant soul be lost or a perverse one preserved.

FOR STUDY AND DISCUSSION

1. How is the doctrine of original sin related to Jeremiah's teaching concerning depravity?
2. List some areas where the common conscience of your community differs from what the Bible teaches.
3. Does the New Testament teach the restoration of Israel as a
political state?

CHAPTER 7 OUTLINE

I. DIVINE JUDGMENT UPON POLITICAL LEADERS (22:1 to 23:8)

II. CONTROVERSIES WITH RELIGIOUS LEADERS (23:9 to 29:32)

7

Conflict with Authority

Jeremiah 22:1 to 29:32; 37–38

THE INNER TENSIONS that wracked Jeremiah were matched by
his constant battle with the authorities of his day. His most
dramatic words are recorded in chapters 22–29, with chapter
21 prefixed to the section as an explanation of Jeremiah's un-
flinching position. It is apparent in this section that the
prophet has indeed become "an iron pillar, and brasen walls"
(1:18).

I. DIVINE JUDGMENT UPON POLITICAL LEADERS (22:1 to 23:8)

Gathered together in this first section are Jeremiah's oracles
concerning the various kings of the period. He had a fitting
word for each one.

1. *Jeremiah and Josiah* (22:10, 15–16)

The writer of the books of Kings is lavish in his praise of
Josiah: "And like unto him was there no king before him,
that turned to the Lord with all his heart, and with all his
soul, and with all his might, according to all the law of
Moses; neither after him arose there any like him" (2 Kings
23:25). In all probability Jeremiah shared this opinion of
the great king, for he was conspicuous among those who
mourned the passing of the godly monarch (2 Chron. 35:
25). In addressing Jehoiakim, Jeremiah paid tribute to his
father: "Did not thy father eat and drink, and do judgment
and justice, and then it was well with him? He judged the
cause of the poor and needy; then it was well with him: was
not this to know me? saith the Lord" (22:15–16). Here the

prophet described Josiah as a man who enjoyed the simple pleasures of life but also stood for integrity and righteousness. He was a true example of the ideal king.

2. The Fate of Jehoahaz (22:10–12)

Although Jeremiah was grief-stricken over the untimely death of Josiah, he was even more heartbroken over young Jehoahaz. After having ruled for only three months, Jehoahaz had been taken to Egypt. Jeremiah clearly saw that the exile was permanent. Shallum (Jehoahaz) would never return to Israel.

It is a pathetic scene when a young man enjoys the center of the stage for a moment and then is ushered unceremoniously into oblivion. In many ways it is better that he had not known notoriety. Athletes who know their fleeting moments of public acclaim are frequently men most to be pitied in later years.

Thinking of the youth who must forever look back upon what had been, Jeremiah ceased grieving for Josiah, who had known a full and rich life, and began to weep for Shallum.

3. The Destiny of Jehoiakim (22:13–19)

Jeremiah saved his most biting sarcasm for the wicked Jehoiakim, who thought that the mark of a great king was the kind of palace in which he dwelt. It meant nothing to him that he had built his house by forced labor and exacted his wealth by oppression. Although he was not interested in justice, the Almighty certainly is. There would be no mourning when Jehoiakim passed on, as was universally true at the death of Josiah. Everyone would be overjoyed to see him go. He would not even be given a decent burial but would be cast outside the city gates, like the abandoned carcass of an ass.

This prophecy presents serious difficulties to the student.[1] Second Kings 24:6 says that Jehoiakim "slept with his fathers," an expression that usually meant burial in the family burial ground. There is no mention either in Kings or Chronicles of a violent death that came to him. The historians seldom overlook a chance to verify prophecies.

Did Jeremiah's prediction fail to be fulfilled literally? This is possible, but it is more likely that Jehoiakim did meet with a violent death by assassination. The Babylonian crisis and a hearty dislike for Jehoiakim probably led influential men in the palace to dispose of him in favor of his eighteen-year-old son, Jehoiachin. Although the expression "slept with his fathers" usually does imply burial in the family burial ground, it is often used of death in general. No convincing arguments can be given to establish a peaceful death for Jehoiakim. In light of this, the Jeremiah passage should be assumed to be eventually verified in history.[2] No matter how he died, one can be sure that he had little peace of soul after his encounter with Jeremiah!

4. God's Wrath upon Jehoiachin (22:24-30)

Young Jehoiachin was doomed through no fault of his own. The sins of his fathers were now being visited upon the children. Nothing could save the city now. Jehoiakim had sown the wind, and his son was reaping the whirlwind. Even if Jehoiachin (Coniah) were God's signet ring, God would still throw him away, Jeremiah asserted. The signet ring was the ancient monarch's sign of authority. It bore his official insignia and was used to make impressions upon the wax of

---

[1] Cf. James Philip Hyatt, "Jeremiah," *The Interpreter's Bible* (Nashville: Abingdon Press, 1956), V, 983–984.

[2] Cf. John Bright, *A History of Israel* (Philadelphia: The Westminster Press, 1959), p. 306.

official documents. It was the last possession a king wished to lose.

Jehoiachin also would go into exile, but in the opposite direction from Egypt, to which Jehoahaz had been taken. There he would be counted as childless, for although children might be born to him, none of his descendants would ever rule upon the throne of David. It would be as if he had no children.

This prophecy also has been the object of much discussion among scholars. It is significant that Jesus legally was a descendant of Jehoiachin. In Matthew 1:11 the Jechonias who is mentioned is the same as Jehoiachin. Jesus, as the Messiah of Israel, is certainly to be understood as the reigning heir of David's line. Was Jeremiah's prophecy invalidated by history?

Apparently what happened is an example of Jeremiah's own description of conditional prophecy (18:5–10). If events had proceeded according to the pattern before Jeremiah, the prophecy would have been fulfilled literally. Evidently, however, the faithfulness of Zerubbabel, who led the restored community of exiles, resulted in a change from the curse to the blessing for his branch of the family of Jehoiachin. It is striking to hear the prophet Haggai saying to Zerubbabel that God would make him his signet, his chosen vessel (Hag. 2:23). Just as Jehoiakim's sin led to the discarding of his son as a useless vessel, just so the faithfulness of Zerubbabel had led God to restore his family to its old position with him.

We can be sure that all this would have been a delight to Jeremiah. He would have much preferred to see Jehoiachin's line purified and restored instead of being abandoned as a total loss. Jeremiah spoke of the future as far as he could see it. The restoration of Jehoiachin's line did not invalidate the prophetic word. Rather, it vindicated the essential ethical principles upon which Jeremiah had built his ministry. God is not bound by arbitrary laws. He acts freely in response to the conduct of free men. No man is doomed to be lost who will turn in faith to the God of grace. All mankind, even as Coniah, is under the curse of God. That does not mean, however, that we must remain under it. We are its victims only as long as we do what comes naturally. When once we turn our eyes above in true repentance, the blessings of God always replace his wrath.

5. *Jeremiah and Zedekiah* (23:6; 21; 37–38)

In 23:6 Jeremiah made a play upon Zedekiah's name, which means "the Lord is righteous." Elsewhere his estimate of Judah's last king may be found. Chapter 21 gives the setting for an understanding of the climactic situation in which these two men were interrelated. Jerusalem was under siege by the Babylonians, and Zedekiah was desperately trying to defend the city. Everyone was being called to the ultimate sacrifice, even of life itself if necessary. Into this tense situation before all the people, Jeremiah threw his explosive words, "Behold, I set before you the way of life, and the way of death. He that abideth in this city shall die by the sword, and by the famine, and by the pestilence: but he that goeth out, and falleth to the Chaldeans that besiege you, he shall live, and his life shall be unto him for a prey" (21:8–9). This would be treason in any land. It is a wonder that Jeremiah escaped with his life. On the contrary, Zedekiah appeared to respect him greatly and secretly seemed to believe that the prophet was right.

Jeremiah's stand makes it clear that the greatest patriot is not always the one that marches when the bugles blow. The truest citizen is the man who takes his stand for what he thinks is best for his beloved land. This kind of courage is not always popular and seldom earns a man distinguished service awards. Yet the future will show that the nation would have been wise to follow the course he pointed out.

Fortunate indeed is that nation which listens to the voice of its men of conviction, yet rare are the countries that have heeded. Israel did not heed.

Like so many leaders today, Zedekiah respected his preacher and wanted to follow his counsel. Chapters 37-38 give an intimate picture of his relationship to Jeremiah.

(1) *He asked his minister to pray for him* (37:3).—Zedekiah was not at all sure of his own ability to reach the ear of God, but he respected Jeremiah enough to ask for his intercession. Yet what he desired was that God would give him success in his undertaking and remove the Chaldeans from the city. He wanted the prophet to use his influence to get God to serve the ends of the state. Apparently Jeremiah was not inclined to do so, for no mention is made of his praying for Zedekiah. The purpose of prayer is to seek for God's will rather than to influence him to reinforce our own plans. The prophet replied to the king that he had talked with the Lord but the divine words reiterated the original declaration to Zedekiah. The city was doomed.

(2) *Zedekiah was anxious to know what God said.*—Zedekiah, however, like so many people, kept hoping that God would change his mind and see the situation the way the king viewed it. He did not want to fight God, as did Jehoiakim. Instead, he was eager to see God on his side. Like the weather, given time enough, God would change his direction, the King thought. In the trouble that followed he was anxious to know what God said (37:17).

There are many people who attend church regularly and are eager to hear a prophetic sermon, yet they never do anything about it. They seem to find satisfaction simply in sitting through it all. To have listened to words of doom and condemnation is penance enough.

(3) *Zedekiah was afraid of what others would say.*—Zedekiah, having heard the truth, did not have the courage to act upon it. He believed what Jeremiah was saying; he could say

amen to every word. If he were living today he would be saying to his pastor, "That's right, preacher." Why, then, did he not act upon his conviction? Zedekiah was just like his counterparts today: he was afraid of what others would do and say (38:19). Jeremiah assured him that he would be safer in the arms of God than with his own plans. Instead of being afraid of other men, he should be mortally afraid of the wrath of God. If a man must fear, let him fear God rather than men. On the contrary, many political leaders are more concerned about public opinion than divine approval. This expedient path may win temporary acclaim but eventually will doom any nation.

6. The Messianic Branch (23:1-8)

There are many scholars who deny this passage to Jeremiah.[3] However, they do not present sufficient evidence to support their position. The burden of the proof must always rest upon those who would deny a passage to its traditional author. The fact that a play is made upon Zedekiah's name would indicate that Jeremiah is the author. Since all the other kings under whom he prophesied are singled out, it would be strange if he had nothing to say in this section about Zedekiah. If 23:6 is not from Jeremiah, there is no reference to Zedekiah at all in this section.

Jeremiah had little to say about the messianic king in contrast to the abundant passages in Isaiah. He had become so disillusioned about the monarchy that he was not disposed toward thinking too much about its future. In this section, however, he reveals that he was confident of the eventual success of the covenant with David. He coined a word for the ideal king, one that formerly had no such significance. The word translated "Branch" is literally a sprout or a shoot (23:5). "Judah was facing a prospect bleak and arid indeed.

---

[3] Cf. John Skinner, *Prophecy and Religion* (Cambridge: The University Press, 1948), pp. 312-313.

But the prophet was sustained by an unshakable confidence in the righteousness of God. In due time the dried-up twig of David's dynasty would put forth a 'Shoot.'" [4]

This future king would be the true Zedekiah (23:6). The name Zedekiah means "the Lord is righteous." The Branch will have a name symbolizing that "the Lord is our righteousness" (Hebrew, *zidekenu*). His coming will mean that the righteousness of the Lord has been communicated to his people.

Against the background of the failure one by one of each member of the Davidic monarchy, Jeremiah saw that one day Israel's God would provide a ruler who would confirm the covenant with David. The prophet did not know how it would be done, but he was convinced that no man could achieve this integrity of character unless the righteousness of the Lord was in him. This one, in turn, would communicate this divine righteousness to his people.

A Christian can never read this prophecy without realizing that Jesus Christ is its fulfilment. He it was, in the fulness of time, who brought the righteousness of God to man. It is he who rules forever as the heir of the promise to David.

II. Controversies with Religious Leaders (23:9 to 29:32)

Buried in the heart of the book of Jeremiah are some of the most significant teachings of the prophet. Here is recorded the account of his conflicts with his contemporaries among the prophets. Theirs was a life or death struggle for the hearts and minds of men, even as today conflicting philosophies challenge the loyalties of all who will heed.

1. *The False Prophets*

These men were never actually called false prophets, for their contemporaries could not always tell them from the

---

[4] H. T. Kuist, "Jeremiah, Lamentations," *The Layman's Bible Commentary* (Richmond, Virginia: John Knox Press, 1960), XII, 71.

true prophets. Many of them were quite sincere in their opinions and spoke with assurance that the Lord had given them their message. Yet history has shown that what Jeremiah said about them was true. They spoke from "their own heart, and not out of the mouth of the Lord" (23:16). Concerning them, God has spoken: "I have not sent these prophets, yet they ran: I have not spoken to them, yet they prophesied. . . . They are prophets of the deceit of their own heart" (23:21, 26).

Every religious community has been plagued by the presence of such a group of ministers. Some of these men delude themselves, and others confuse the people with lies (23:22). An awareness of this fact should warn each minister to guard his own heart and each layman to protect his own pulpit.

2. The Marks of a True Prophet

Out of his struggle with those who challenged the validity of his own message, Jeremiah learned how to tell the difference between a true and a false prophet. His principles are of great value to those who are perplexed today by the conflicting claims of rival philosophies. In this section he points out the characteristics of a true prophet of God.

(1) *The true prophet possesses high moral standards* (23:9-19, 22).—The true prophet always seeks to turn people from their sinful ways, instead of encouraging them to continue in them (23:22). The message that he preaches contains "words of his [the Lord's] holiness" (23:9). The true prophet's personal life stands behind his words. He never would say, "Do not do as I do, but do as I say." In contrast to him, the false prophet is profane (polluted, opposite of holy) and wicked (23:11). The faithful prophet never equates right with might (23:10b). He recognizes that often the majority may not be right. Dedicated to decency, he will do nothing to strengthen the bonds of evildoers (23:14). No

man is a true prophet of God who is not himself morally pure, both in example and precept.

(2) *The true prophet makes accurate predictions* (23:20–23).—God is aware of what is ahead for his people (23:23), and a prophet who is in his inner counsel will be given something of this divine knowledge. What others will understand only after it has happened, he will be able to anticipate (23:20). There are some scholars who have contended that the predictive element in Old Testament prophecy is a minor one. Yet there is no more certain test of the validity of a prophet's message than the outcome of history (Deut. 18:21–22).

(3) *The divinely inspired prophet will have an effective ministry* (23:28–29).—Jeremiah challenged his rivals to preach their dreams and see what would happen. If they were from God their words would remain like grains of wheat after the chaff was blown away. Faithful preaching is like a fire devouring stubble or a hammer breaking rock into pieces. Jeremiah did not mean by this that the prophet would necessarily attain worldly recognition, but he did mean that he would accomplish his purpose. He might be rejected, but he never could be ignored.

(4) *His message will have vitality* (23:33–40).—Every prophet in Jeremiah's day began his oracle with the phrase, "The burden of the Lord." This gave it a note of authority. Jeremiah contended that too frequent usage had destroyed the significance of the phrase. He suggested that they use substitute phrases that would be meaningful to the people (23:35). Religion must be kept always fresh and vital. The old truths must be expressed in a language that each generation can understand.

(5) *The true prophet is cautious* (23:32).—The true prophet will not be too quick to come to a conclusion. The word translated "lightness" is from a root that means to leap or bound, and the noun consequently pictures a man

who too readily jumps to conclusions. The inspired man will carefully weigh his conclusions before he brings them to the people.

(6) *He preaches judgment upon sin* (chaps. 24–26).—In 28:8–9, Jeremiah summarized this truth. Chapters 24–26 contain examples of this type of preaching from Jeremiah. In chapter 24 Jeremiah refuted the popular opinion in Jerusalem that those taken in captivity in the year 597 deserved it while those left behind were approved of God. "You," said Jeremiah to his audience, "are the bad figs, and God will throw you away." Chapter 25 contains the prophet's denunciations both upon Judah and all the nations of the earth. They all must drink of the divine "cup of this fury" (25:15–29). Babylon's supremacy was limited to seventy years (25:12), after which she, too, would go down under the wrath of God. Chapter 26 has already been discussed in chapter 3 of this study. It contains the record of Jeremiah's condemnation of the Temple and the sacrificial system.

(7) *Finally, the inspired prophet has faith in the future* (29:1–14).—Although Jeremiah saw no chance of relief for the present, he was confident of the future, for God would not rest until his will for his people was realized (29:11–14). The real prophet is often overwhelmed with despair when he looks about him, but his faith always looks up to God.

FOR STUDY AND DISCUSSION

1. Should the Christian be interested in politics? What are his responsibilities as a citizen?
2. Are we, like Jehoahaz and Jehoiachin, suffering for the sins of our fathers? In what areas is this true? Is it right that it should be so?
3. What factors lead a man to become a false prophet? How can he avoid or overcome them?

CHAPTER 8 OUTLINE

I. THE SOURCE OF TRUE OPTIMISM (30:1 to 31:26)
1. Cause for Pessimism
2. Cause for Optimism

II. THE NEW COVENANT (31:27–34)
1. The Basis of the Covenant
2. The Nature of the Covenant

III. FAITH AND CIRCUMSTANCE (32:1–44)
1. The Vision
2. The Actual Scene
3. Jeremiah's Dutiful Behavior
4. The Rising of Doubt
5. The Reassurance of God

IV. ENTERING THE FORTRESS OF GOD (33:1–26)
1. God's Truths Are Guarded
2. Truths Revealed to Jeremiah

8

Hope for the Future

Jeremiah 30:1 to 33:26

No MORE STIRRING PASSAGES ever were written than those found in this section of Jeremiah. Although most of his messages concerned judgment and doom, when he dreamed of the future he could preach the way he really preferred. All his heart went into these sermons.

I. THE SOURCE OF TRUE OPTIMISM (30:1 to 31:26)

How did it happen that the dejected prophet could have such confidence in the future? It is not easy to hope for a better time when your world has crashed down upon your head. These chapters were probably composed after the fall of Jerusalem in 587 B.C.

1. Cause for Pessimism

There was every reason to despair. Israel had been struck a mortal blow by her God (30:14); the exile had begun. There was no cure for the wound (30:12 to 31:15). Any competent physician would have considered the condition quite hopeless; in fact, no physician would ever have accepted the case. Apparently there was nothing to do but await the hour of death.

2. Cause for Optimism

The pessimist overlooks the most significant fact of all. There is a physician who can help when all others fail. God specializes in the miraculous. He has the ability to effect a cure (30:7), and he does not wait to be summoned. When everyone has given up on the patient, he volunteers his serv-ices. He seeks out the one wounded by his wrath, knowing that at last he will be heeded (31:3).

One of the most beautiful passages in the Old Testament follows, picturing the process through which Israel will be restored, a description of *the journey back to God* (31:4–14). The return will be inaugurated by God himself (31:8a). In whatever condition they may find themselves, they will begin the journey, whether blind, lame, or with child. They will return just as they are (31:8b). At the start they will weep with remorse and beg for mercy (31:9a). When the restora-tion shall have been completed, "their soul shall be as a watered garden" (31:12), like an irrigated field in a desert land.

Now the prophet was disturbed by the sound of weeping. It came from Ramah, in whose vicinity Rachel had been buried after she died in childbirth. Indeed it was Rachel her-self weeping, refusing to be comforted because she had lost all her children. Her travail had been in vain, for Israel was no more (31:15). God proceeded to quiet her, answering her that her children would one day come back home. She need grieve no more (31:16–17).

Until now Jeremiah has emphasized how God feels toward his helpless people. In an instructive passage (31:18–20) he gives insight into the pardoned sinner's heart, who cries out in sincere repentance. He realizes now that the chastise-ments of God were sent to teach him the facts of life. As the bullock is struck by his master to train him to pull a load, just so adversity teaches a man to assume his responsibilities under God. Whatever way God desires to turn him, he is ready to go. Through suffering he has learned to submit to the will of God (31:18).

After God has turned him from his stubborn way, he re-pents (Hebrew, "feels sorry"); after he has been taught, he smites his thigh in disgust (31:19). These verbs seem to be in the wrong order. Usually one repents and then turns from sin; he feels convicted of his sins, and then submits to God's teaching. Here the order is reversed. Although the usual order is a necessary part of an experience with God, yet the present arrangement is quite instructive. Although one repents when he first comes to God, he cannot really see how terrible his sin is until after he leaves it. He thinks that he hates his sin when he first forsakes it, but afterward he is even more amazed than ever at the stupidity of sin. He sees more than ever that he has deserved all the chastisement that has come to him; he has been a perverse teen-ager (31:19). This sincere repentance brings a ready response from God. Like a compassionate father, all the time that he was forced to discipline his child his heart was bleeding. Now that the lad's attitude has changed he can restore him to favor (31:20).

As Israel returns to her land, she is to set up signposts along the way, piles of rock that mark the road home (31:21). One scholar suggests that the passage be regarded as spurious, since the traveler does not put up highway signs but follows them. What Jeremiah had in mind, however, was that the first to travel the road should mark the way for those who would follow. Those who take the way of life today should make it easier for those who follow after them.

This section closes with a difficult oracle: "The Lord hath created a new thing in the earth, A woman shall compass a man" (31:22). The literal Hebrew reads, "A woman shall encircle a man." There are many interpretations given this passage. Some understand the verb to have the sense of "conquer," hence "a woman shall conquer a man"; the weaker shall conquer the stronger. This would mean that Israel, a weak nation, would overcome the stronger ones about her. Bernard Duhm suggests that the sentence is a scribal gloss. Some interpreter was reading the passage when he noticed an amusing situation. Israel was referred to as a son in 31:20, whereas in 31:22 that nation is a daughter. So the reader wrote in the margin his reaction to this change in sex: "God has made a new creation, he has changed a woman into a man." This comment was never meant to be in the text, but someone copied it by mistake. This view is intriguing, but must be rejected for two reasons: It necessitates a correction in the Hebrew text (from "encircle" to "change"); and it is pure conjecture.

A third alternative is probably the correct one. The verb can be read "protect." This would mean that the land is so well defended by God that even a woman could fight off any attack. While her husband is working in the fields, he can be protected by his wife, who is given divine strength. Regardless of what the passage meant in Jeremiah's day, it has certainly been fulfilled today. Through the freedom given her by the influence of the Christian faith, woman is not always the weaker vessel. Although a real man would not hide behind a woman's skirts, if he needs protection he can certainly receive it!

II. THE NEW COVENANT (31:27–34)

Of all the sayings of Jeremiah these are without doubt the most significant. It is this passage that Jesus had in mind when he instituted the Lord's Supper (Matt. 26:28). The expression "new testament" literally means new covenant. In other words, Jesus was saying that the new covenant predicted by Jeremiah was now being instituted. He could think of no better term to describe his work of salvation. The apostle Paul used this passage as the basis for his contrast between the old dispensation and the new (2 Cor. 3:1–18). The writer of Hebrews gave a lengthy application of the significance of the words of Jeremiah (8:8 ff.).

When the early Christians faced the decision of naming the new Scriptures, the choice was obvious. The Jewish Scriptures would be called The Old Covenant (Testament) and the Christian writings The New Covenant (Testament).

Thus the very names of the two sections of the Bible are a testimony to the insight of Jeremiah. This "not only bears witness to the clearness of Jeremiah's spiritual perception in an age of almost universal religious darkness, but also provides a striking illustration of the unity of the Scriptures in their presentation of God's way of life for sinful men." [1]

1. *The Basis of the Covenant*

Two matters are basic in the understanding of the new covenant. Jeremiah mentioned them in the preface to the covenant itself (31:27-30). First in importance is the intention of God (31:27-28). He is determined to restore Israel and has set his mind to this purpose. The second fact is that in any dealings with Israel, God will work with individuals. Each person will be held responsible only for his own sins (31:29-30). He will not be able to blame his eventual fate upon anyone except himself. This is always the manner in which the Lord has dealt with men, but Jeremiah was one of the first to see it. We suffer because of the sins of our fathers, but we are not held responsible for them, as in the case of Achan's family when he sinned at Jericho (Josh. 7:22-25).

2. *The Nature of the Covenant*

The new covenant will not be made until after Israel shall have been restored to its land (31:33). Thus it "lies yet in a later stage of development. We stand here in the sphere of eschatology. Man of himself is not able to fulfill the divine commandment." [2] In the fulness of time God himself will make the ideal life possible.

Some scholars doubt that Jeremiah is the author of this

---

[1] Alexander Stewart, *Jeremiah* (Edinburgh: W. F. Henderson, 1936), pp. 203-204.

[2] Elmer A. Leslie, *Jeremiah* (New York: Abingdon Press, 1954), p. 107.

passage. "Covenant," they contend, is a legalistic term and is unworthy of Jeremiah the mystic. On the contrary, Jeremiah was using a legal term as a vehicle to convey a deeper spiritual truth. He revitalized the idea. This concept is a natural outgrowth of his own experience and theology. "His knowledge of the abounding guilt and spiritual impotence of men forced him—speaking from the human point of view—to look for a way of deliverance in which grace would much more abound. So his doctrine of the new covenant is the correlative of his doctrine of human sin." [3] There can be no other solution to the depravity of man. What the new covenant promises is "not sinlessness, but forgiveness." [4] God will provide a way for sinful man to be reconciled to him—a way that will enable him to walk with God while he is conquering his sinfulness.

The new covenant is contrasted with the old in several striking ways.

(1) *The success of this covenant is guaranteed by God.*— It is significant to contrast the verbs in the Ten Commandments of the old covenant (Ex. 20) with those in this passage. There we read "thou shalt," and "thou shalt not." Here we see "I will put . . . and write," and "I will forgive." It is clear that the success of the old agreement was dependent upon Israel's ability to keep it. This she could not do. Why, then, was it made with her? To lead her to see the necessity of the new one. Man would never accept grace if he thought he could deserve the favor of God. And he thinks he deserves it until he comes to see his own helplessness.

The old covenant revealed Israel's inability to meet God's requirements. When this covenant was first made, she thought she could keep her side of it. It took long centuries of tragic failure to prepare her for the new one. Even after the

---

[3] Alexander Stewart, *op. cit.*, p. 37.

[4] Cf. J. Philip Hyatt, *Jeremiah: Prophet of Courage and Hope* (New York: Abingdon Press, 1958), p. 107.

exile she thought the renewal of the old was sufficient. In the times of Jesus the average Jew had still not learned, nor does he yet see, the necessity of a new relation to God. Jeremiah, therefore, not only saw beyond the horizon of his own day but saw more than his fellow Hebrews can understand today.

(2) *The new covenant is the ultimate in grace.*—The first covenant forgave the sin of Israel, but the second even pardoned the breaking of the first covenant itself. "It forgave the breach which had destroyed the old." [5] It is one thing for a man to overlook the sins of his wife before he marries her and quite another to forgive her when she sins against their own marriage vows.

(3) *The impulse to keep it comes from within.*—It is written on the heart rather than on tables of stone (31:33). The old covenant emphasized "a forced submission to an external authority." [6] Obedience under the new would issue from personal desire rather than a sense of duty. Man would serve God because it was what he wanted to do, rather than just because he ought. By the painful process of his own frustrations Jeremiah had come to realize the necessity of this kind of experience.

(4) *This new covenant is to be an individual matter* (31:34).—Each person must have his own encounter with God. Personal faith cannot be taught as one can teach a law that is written on a stone. It must be experienced to be real. Jeremiah did not mean that there would be no place for teachers under this new covenant. There will always be a need for them. Their function, however, will be to lead people to the conviction that they must have an experience with God to be under covenant, and after they are within it, to help them see the implications of the faith. All those within the covenant, however, will of necessity have had a personal experi-

---

[5] A. C. Welch, *Jeremiah*, p. 230.

[6] Alexander Stewart, *op. cit.*, p. 38.

ence with God. "The only thing which men cannot hand on in this world is their experience." [7]

There is no mention of the place of the Gentiles by Jeremiah, but since it is an individual affair, it could hardly be limited to Israel. Yet so far as he was concerned, Israel was the recipient of the covenant. It is a sober reminder of our human frailty to see Jeremiah at the moment of his highest inspiration still limited in his view of God's all-inclusiveness. How easy it is to be interested only in our own, and how difficult to make the world our parish! The "prophet to the nations" is more concerned about their destruction than their salvation.

(5) *The permanence of this covenant.*—The final contrast between the old and the new is the permanence of this covenant. The old one was broken over and over again, but the new one will last. The old conditions are no more. God himself guarantees the outcome of this relationship to him. The New Testament doctrine of salvation is based solidly upon this truth. The man who knows Jesus Christ as personal Lord and Saviour has a relationship with God that will endure forever. For such a man to be lost would mean that God had not kept his covenant.

III. FAITH AND CIRCUMSTANCE (32:1–44)

There come times in every man's life when outward circumstances discourage faith. Jeremiah was in such a situation. Nebuchadnezzar's armies were already encamped around the city, and the prophet was "shut up in the court of the prison" (32:2), having even exasperated Zedekiah himself (32:3). If ever he would take a dim view of the future, it would be now.

1. *The Vision*

Jeremiah had a vision in which he was informed by God

[7] A. C. Welch, *loc. cit.*

that Hanameel, his cousin, was coming to offer him a chance to buy a field in Anathoth, which was up for sale (32:6-7). Jeremiah was first in line for the property. The prophet was not told what he was to do about the offer. It was a strange time to buy that field, for the Babylonian armies were probably encamped upon it at the time!

2. *The Actual Scene*

Just as God had said, Hanameel came to him and made the offer. When this happened, Jeremiah knew that God was in it (32:8). Apparently he had not been too sure before. Although God had required strange things of him previously, this was quite incredible. Buy a field in Anathoth during the siege? Only a fool would do that.

3. *Jeremiah's Dutiful Behavior*

Jeremiah knew what God expected of him, for he would not have informed him beforehand unless he had wanted him to transact the business. So the prophet weighed out the money, since coined money was not in use. The seventeen shekels of silver weighed about seven ounces. It is impossible to tell whether he paid an exorbitant price or not, since the size of the field and the value of land at the time are not known. Any price at all, however, was too much.

The procedure that followed is an eyewitness' account of how business was carried on at the time. A single piece of papyrus parchment was used for the deed, the record being inscribed both at the top and the bottom of it, a space being left between the two inscriptions. The upper portion was rolled and sealed as the official document, and the lower left open for anyone to read. This, in turn, was placed in an earthen vessel to preserve it until the land became of value again (32:14-15). It was such a jar as this in which the Dead Sea Scrolls were preserved so many centuries. Perhaps some day Jeremiah's deed will be found!

4. *The Rising of Doubt*

No sooner had Jeremiah performed his duty than his doubts began to come. What a stupid thing to do! God had performed many miracles in the past (32:16-22), and now had fulfilled his word in bringing Nebuchadnezzar. The city would soon fall, and the nation be destroyed. How could the land ever be worth anything again (32:25)? In times of stress the Christian knows what he ought to do and say and may dutifully carry out his responsibilities. Yet this does not keep honest doubts from arising. It is significant that the prophet did not publish his doubts but rather he prayed about them.

5. *The Reassurance of God*

In replying to Jeremiah the Lord used the same words he had uttered in his prayer. The answer might be paraphrased as follows: "You just said that nothing is too hard for me (32:17). Do you really believe that (32:27)? If I could bring up Israel out of Egypt, surely I can bring them back from Babylon. The purpose of the captivity is not to destroy my people but to redeem them" (32:42). Verses 38-41 treat the same theme as 31:31-34, yet in a little different way. The restored people will inhabit their land once more, and land will once again be valuable. They will be given "one heart, and one way" (32:39). This combination is still difficult to find. Rare indeed does a situation exist where people not only have the same purposes, but also agree upon how they should be achieved. Only the presence of the Spirit of God can guarantee such behavior. This time God will give himself without reservation, "with my whole heart and with my whole soul" (32:41). How else could this be fulfilled except in the incarnation?

IV. ENTERING THE FORTRESS OF GOD (33:1–26)

This passage deals with the necessity of prayer if one is to receive the revelation of God. If the prophet will pray with faith, God will show him the secrets of the future. (33:3)

1. *God's Truths Are Guarded*

The word translated "mighty" in verse 3 literally means inaccessible. It is used generally of fortified cities (Num. 13: 28; Deut. 1:28; 3:5; 2 Sam. 20:6; Isa. 2:15), and is often translated as "fenced" or "walled." Jeremiah was told that God's truths are inaccessible to man's own mind. God fences them in and keeps them from the inquiring mind. The only way that these truths can be known is for God to reveal them. The Word of God is given to men by God.

2. *Truths Revealed to Jeremiah*

The prophet prepared his heart to receive God's truth, and it was given to him. When all others about him were in despair, he was led to see that God would keep his covenant with David and Levi. One day God would restore his people to their land and reinstate their Temple worship. The future of God's people was secure, for they were in the hands of the God of grace (33:4–26).

FOR STUDY AND DISCUSSION

1. What is the significance of the term "covenant"? What uses does it have in the Old Testament? How were covenants made?
2. How are the Gentiles related to the new covenant? What problems did this present to the New Testament church?
3. What can you do to show your faith in your church and in its future?

CHAPTER 9 OUTLINE

I. IGNORING THE WORD (34:1–22)
1. The Word Declared
2. The Word Heeded
3. The Easing of the Crisis
4. Convenient Religion Condemned

II. LOYALTY TO THE WORD (35:1–19)
1. The Coming of the Rechabites
2. The Test of Faithfulness
3. Prophetic Application

III. ATTACKING THE WORD (36:1–32)
1. The Purpose of the Word
2. The Word Proclaimed
3. The Destruction of the Scroll
4. The Word Restored

The Indestructible Word of God

Jeremiah 34:1 to 36:32

THIS COLLECTION OF NARRATIVES from various periods of Jeremiah's ministry is grouped around Israel's response to the revealed truths of God. The passages throw significant light upon the consequences of failure to heed the divine admonitions.

I. IGNORING THE WORD (34:1-22)

As the chapter opens, Jeremiah was preaching his usual message to Zedekiah. The city was doomed to destruction and its citizens would go into captivity.

1. *The Word Declared*

Jeremiah fearlessly delivered his word directly to Zedekiah (34:6). Just as the prophet now faced the king, so also Zedekiah would meet Nebuchadnezzar, "eyeball to eyeball, and mouth to mouth" (34:3). However, he would not be executed by the Babylonian monarch. Rather he would be taken into exile and die the slow death of the brokenhearted. Actually Zedekiah was captured as he tried to flee the city and was taken to Nebuchadnezzar, who ordered his sons killed before his eyes and then put out the Hebrew king's eyes with a hot iron. Burned upon those sightless eyeballs was a horrible spectacle that could never be erased.

2. *The Word Heeded*

Frightened Zedekiah was impelled to do something to win back the favor of God. "Zedekiah, the halting, the afraid, the vacillating, under the impulse of some qualm of conscience, had gathered the people together into the temple, . . . and had entered into solemn covenant to give liberty to all those to whom liberty was due." [1] An ancient Hebrew law clearly stated that a Hebrew slave could not be retained longer than six years. In the seventh year he was to go free (Ex. 21:2). In all their history the Jews had paid little or no attention to this law (Jer. 34:14b), but in this crisis they suddenly became concerned. Although Jeremiah's words had profound effect upon Zedekiah, the particular method he chose to demonstrate his good faith was necessitated by the conditions of the siege. The masters were probably afraid of an uprising of the slaves and felt that if they were freed, they would fight with more determination for the city. Thus one move would accomplish a double purpose. It would placate God and remove the danger of a rebellion. Although their motives were mixed, it was a move in the right direction (34:15).

3. *The Easing of the Crisis*

Just after this significant social reform was inaugurated, with the potential of securing the favor of God and the survival of the city, Nebuchadnezzar lifted the siege. Word had come to him of the approach of the Egyptians, and he marched to meet them. It appeared that the danger was over, for what chance would Nebuchadnezzar have in the Pharaoh's own front yard? Accordingly, the owners immediately put their recently emancipated slaves back into bondage (34:11). In other words, when a religious move tended to bring them security they favored it. When there was no personal advantage attached to it, they turned the other way. Religion was a practice to be put on or taken off at their own

[1] G. Campbell Morgan, *Studies in the Prophecy of Jeremiah* (New York: Fleming H. Revell Company, 1931), p. 219.

convenience. This behavior reminded G. Campbell Morgan of some well-known lines:

> The devil was sick, the devil a monk would be;
> The devil got well, the devil a monk was he!
> —RABELAIS

Deathbed repentance is a dubious affair. Many of those expecting to die eventually get well. Their record of reform has not been impressive. People who turn to God under extreme pressure are not as likely to remain continually faithful as those who quietly and resolutely surrender into the hands of God no matter what lies ahead. It is much better that a man make up his mind on his own than that he be pressured into a decision forced upon his unwilling soul.

Left to their own initiative the leaders in Jerusalem would never have freed their slaves. The pressure of the situation, both from God and man, influenced them to act in a pattern foreign to their disposition. Once the pressure was off they went back to their old ways.

4. *Convenient Religion Condemned*

Jeremiah was indignant. In behaving like this the people had polluted the name of the Lord. The word translated "polluted" literally means to bore or to pierce and hence comes to mean to open up or make common. It is obviously the opposite of "to be holy" or "separate." If a people bear the name of God, others judge his nature by their behavior. In two ways they had made the name of God common (like any other god), rather than holy (different) before the world: They had broken a solemn covenant with the Lord (34:15b, 18–19), and they had denied their fellow men the rights that were justly theirs.

Nothing could displease God more then, or now, for his very nature is to effect justice and keep his covenants. Jeremiah expressed his displeasure in graphic language. Since the people had refused to give liberty to their slaves, God had decided to free the people from his own protection (34:17). All that keeps any of us from destruction is the mighty arm of Providence. If God removed his tender care, we would be exposed immediately to all the destructive forces about us—sword, pestilence, and famine. It is not necessary for God to destroy his people. All that is necessary is for him to remove his protection. Their natural enemies will do the rest.

II. LOYALTY TO THE WORD (35:1–19)

During the time when the Babylonians encamped before Jerusalem, Jeremiah took the occasion to teach the people the foolishness of their neglect of the Torah (revelation) of God. Rather than preaching a sermon, he used an object lesson, the participants being a strange group of people who had recently come to stay in the city.

1. *The Coming of the Rechabites*

Politics makes strange bedfellows. The unsettled conditions in Judah had brought a peculiar band into the safety of the city walls. They were the Rechabites, who were homeless, tent-dwelling nomads, opposed to agriculture and the fruit of the vine. Normally they would not have been caught inside a city, but the Babylonian invasion had interrupted their usual pattern of life. They are reminiscent of beliefs of certain religious sects today that are quite satisfying when one is well and prospering but offer little comfort in times of trouble.

These strange fellows were descendants of Rechab, who was a Kenite, a people among whom Moses lived in the wilderness years, and from whom he took a wife. These Rechabites attained notoriety in the days of Jehu, when Jonadab (Jehonadab), the son of Rechab, participated heartily in that king's eradication of Baal worship in Israel (2

Kings 10:15 ff.). Jonadab was a staunch believer in the "old time religion," and to him this meant observing the identical social patterns of his ancestors, as well as the same religious faith. Therefore, he commanded his sons that they should never forsake his own way of life. They must continue to dwell in tents and not plant crops or drink wine. This teaching they had continued to observe for two hundred years without variation (Jer. 35:8-11).

2. *The Test of Faithfulness*

Jeremiah escorted the Rechabites to a side room of the Temple, set wine before them, and urged them to drink it. "Now it must be understood that this was by no means intended as a temptation to them. It was done in order to give them the opportunity to refuse."[2] As Jeremiah expected, they politely turned down the invitation. The wine was no temptation to them whatsoever. Why did they refuse it? Not because it was physically harmful. This issue they had probably never raised. Their ancestor had so instructed them, and they followed him without question. It was not for them to ask whether a matter was right or wrong in itself. If their father taught it, that was sufficient reason for them.

3. *Prophetic Application*

Jeremiah used the occasion to upbraid his fellow Hebrews. The Rechabites had obeyed Jonadab without question for all these years. Yet Israel had no inclination to follow the instruction of the Lord, so carefully given through his prophets (35:12-15). The Rechabites were more faithful to the commandment of a man than God's people were to his teaching. Thus it always has been. Men have been disposed to follow other men whom they can see rather than God, whom they cannot see.

Divine judgment would fall upon Israel for the neglect of

---

[2] G. Campbell Morgan, *op. cit.*, p. 229.

God's word. However, the Rechabites would be blessed for their faithfulness to their traditions, which were godly ones. They were not humanists, worshiping Jonadab, but rather accepted his ideas concerning how God should be worshiped. This was far better than not worshiping God at all, as was true of Israel. Because of this adherence to principle, God promised that "Jonadab the son of Rechab shall not want a man to stand before me for ever" (35:19). The idiom "to stand before me" is used of those who are the servants of God, his priests and prophets. The same expression is used of Jeremiah (15:19).

There could be no greater contrast than that between Jeremiah and the Rechabites. They were traditionalists to the core; Jeremiah was a rebel. Their two viewpoints normally represent hostile religious philosophies. For the Rechabites, whose attitude is reflected in their spiritual heirs of today, the proper way to preserve the faith was to retire from the onrushing stream of life and live the simple way. They kept themselves separate from the world in the sense that no new customs were acceptable. Any new social pattern was not of God. People like this always appear quaint to a progressive society, but they are good, solid citizens who love the Lord. In many ways their simple life is a happier one than that of the man who tries to keep up with the times.

On the other hand, Jeremiah, anticipating the view of Jesus, realized that man cannot successfully ignore social change. Religion must have a word for the men who are caught in the main stream of life. This calls for a turbulent life as one rethinks his religion, remolds opinion, fights the contrary tides of the times, but ultimately reshapes history.

These two groups are often mortal enemies. But if they are sincere followers of God, there is no need for such animosities. The common respect that Jeremiah and the Rechabites had for each other should encourage us today in our fellowship. The common enemy is too strong for God's people to be divided over the nonessentials of the faith.

III. ATTACKING THE WORD (36:1–32)

1. *The Purpose of the Word*

The prophet was told to record his oracles uttered over a period of twenty years that the nation might hear and repent. Jeremiah himself was "shut up" (36:5) and not allowed to preach in public. It is possible that, had he not been so restrained, he would not have written down his message even then, but would have been satisfied with delivering it orally. Perhaps the preservation of his prophecies was due to the very situation that necessitated the calling of Baruch: the restraints placed upon Jeremiah. Just so, John Bunyan might never have written *The Pilgrim's Progress* if he had not been languishing in the Bedford jail.

2. *The Word Proclaimed*

After carefully copying down Jeremiah's dictated words, Baruch read the warnings before the throngs at the Temple and then to a private meeting of some of the nobles (36:6–15), who seemed to be friendly toward Jeremiah (36:16–19). They were evidently the leaders who remained from Josiah's regime. The faithful proclamation of the word resulted in a great stir in the city, as it always does. Preaching even brings life to the dead (Ezek. 37).

3. *The Destruction of the Scroll*

When the scroll was brought to Jehoiakim, he was sitting by an open fire, surrounded by his own courtiers. As the prophecies were read he deliberately cut them into pieces with his penknife and threw them into the fire (36:22–23, 32). Thus he demonstrated his defiance of the laws of God. As the pages turned to ashes, the foolish king thought that their words were nullified.

4. *The Word Restored*

No sooner did the news reach Jeremiah that the scroll had been burned than he began to redictate its content to Baruch. And to it were added many similar words of wrath (36:27–32). The attempt of Jehoiakim to destroy the word of God had not only ended in total failure but had also resulted in a stronger condemnation than ever for him and his followers.

Today men have learned that they can never destroy the Bible by open attack. History is too full of witnesses to the contrary. Now its greatest enemies are either those who pretend to be its friends or who as its friends become its most dangerous foes. On the one hand, "It is mutilated in the house of its friends, and its claim to be the very Word of God is dismissed as the survival of an antiquated doctrine of inspiration." [3] On the other hand, even more dangerous to its survival are those who still believe it to be the Word of God but who find no place for it in their hearts and lives. To believe the Bible is to live by it. It is not enough to take it to Sunday school and deposit it on the desk. Its words must live in our hearts.

FOR STUDY AND DISCUSSION

1. What are the advantages and dangers of "high-pressure" evangelism?
2. Into what theological groups would modern Baptists be classified? Is it possible for them to respect one another?
3. What dangers beset the Bible today? What will be the outcome?
4. Is the Bible the word of man as well as the Word of God? What are the implications of this?

---

[3] Alexander Stewart, *op. cit.*, p. 237.

Suggestions to the Teachers

THERE IS NOTHING quite so important for the teacher as being prepared. The author once asked an eminent scholar in the field of education what he considered to be the ideal method of teaching. He replied that, in his opinion, it was the discussion method, with the leader guiding the meeting of minds in a planned direction. Then someone wanted to know if he considered Jesus a good teacher. "Why, certainly," he replied. "He was the Master Teacher." Then came the inquiry, "What method did he use?" The specialist hesitated a moment, then answered, "He used many methods, but his favorite was to tell a story or pronounce an oracle, then answer the questions arising from the issues raised." "Why then," the questioner wanted to know, "shouldn't we use the same method?" Quick was the reply, "The difference is that Jesus had something to say!"

Whether the teacher should use the lecture and question method or the discussion and conclusions method is a matter of opinion. Whatever approach is employed, however, it is a good idea for the teacher to have something to say. What he reads will vitally affect his knowledge. The following books will prove helpful, depending upon the need of the teacher or his particular interest.

1. For an accurate survey of the history of the period of Jeremiah's ministry, John Bright's *A History of Israel* is by far the most reliable study.

2. In expository studies, works on Jeremiah are particularly numerous and helpful, although few are of recent date. G. Campbell Morgan, *Studies in the Prophecy of Jeremiah,* is second to none. Although a brief work, Wheeler Robinson's *The Cross of Jeremiah* is most rewarding, as well as T. C. Gordon's *The Rebel Prophet.* Alexander Stewart's *Jeremiah, the Man and His Message* will arouse the reader's imagination and give him some of the prophet's spark of inspiration. Of the more recent works, Fred M. Wood's *Fire in My Bones* especially excels.

3. For more serious study the following are recommended: A. C. Welch, *Jeremiah, His Time and His Work;* John Skinner, *Prophecy and Religion;* and James Philip Hyatt's study in *The Interpreter's Bible.*

In planning the emphases of the various discussion periods, it may be pointed out that several approaches can be made, depending upon local or personal factors.

If particular interest is to be centered on the message of Jeremiah to an age in turmoil, his book has much to say. There are similarities in world tensions and moral and spiritual weakness among responsible people. On the local scene, Jeremiah's message affects political, religious, and social issues. He spoke out courageously in all three areas.

If the emphasis desired is theological, every major area of debate is involved—free will and predestination, depravity and the new birth, prophecy and fulfilment, institutionalism and personal faith, education and revelation.

For those who prefer the personal application, Jeremiah is particularly rich in the light he throws upon the peculiar problems of religious people: the conflict between the will of God and personal desire, the value of personal communion in prayer, overcoming sensitiveness to criticism, learning to live alone whether one likes it or not, the proper attitude toward other believers.

Above everything, let the teacher resolve in all of his planning that, whatever the approach pursued, he shall have as his purpose but one primary objective: that when the study is over everyone shall remember not so much the leader or the discussions as the fact that Jeremiah came alive and spoke anew. This time, however, he was not rejected but received with open hearts.

Suggested Audio-Visual Aids
for Teaching This Book

I. HISTORICAL BACKGROUND MATERIALS

SLIDES

N 101, *Josiah Hearing the Words of the Law* (53s)

Ha 699, *King Josiah Told About the Newly Found Books of the Law* (2 Kings 22:10) (53s)

Ha 700, *Shapan Reads the Book of the Law to Josiah* (2 Kings 22:10–11) (53s)

FILMSTRIPS

The Temples of the Pharaohs, 41 frames, color, with manual, (73m) $6.00, recording, $2.95

Egypt and the Bible, 43 frames, color, with manual, (73m) $6.00, recording, $2.95

Babylon, the Glory of Kingdoms, 26 frames, color, with manual, (73m) $6.00, recording, $2.95

II. THE PROPHET JEREMIAH

SLIDES

N 102, *Jeremiah in the Stocks* (Jer. 20:2) (53s)

N 103, *Jeremiah Taken Out of the Dungeon* (53s)

Ha 702, *Jeremiah Rescued from the Mob* (Jer. 26:8–17) (53s)

Ha 703, *Jeremiah Saved by King Zedekiah* (53s)

FILMSTRIP

The Rebel Prophet is a Broadman filmstrip prepared especially for use with this book. It could be used in advance of the study to create interest. It could be used with the first chapter on the first night of the study as an introduction. Other teachers may prefer to use only the frames that relate to the chapters studied each night; others will prefer to use the filmstrip the concluding session as a summary. Any single use or combination of uses of the filmstrip will make the study more meaningful.

OTHER RELATED FILMSTRIPS

A Cry for Repentance—Jeremiah, 30 frames, color, with manual, (53s) $5.00

Jeremiah—The Reluctant Rebel, 54 frames, color, with manual, (66c) $6.00, recording, $3.00

Questions for Review and
Written Work

FOR INSTRUCTIONS concerning the written work and the requesting of awards, see "Requirements for Credit in Class or Home Study," page ix.

CHAPTER 1

1. Name the kings of Judah during the ministry of Jeremiah.
2. List the principal events from 626 B.C. until 587 B.C.
3. Is the title "weeping prophet" appropriate for Jeremiah?
4. Name the seven major divisions of the book of Jeremiah.

CHAPTER 2

5. Contrast the calls of Jeremiah and Isaiah.
6. What earlier prophet had a strong influence on Jeremiah?
7. What nation did Jeremiah have in mind in his oracles of doom?

CHAPTER 3

8. Whose prophecies encouraged the Temple superstition?
9. Where was the sanctuary located during the time of Eli?
10. What externals did Jeremiah predict would be destroyed because of Israel's sin?

CHAPTER 4

11. What verse was probably used to combat idolatry during the exile?
12. Why is idolatry stupid?
13. What is true wisdom?

CHAPTER 5

14. What were some reasons for Jeremiah's personal conflicts?
15. How are Jeremiah's curses on his enemies to be understood?
16. How did Jeremiah settle his personal problems?

CHAPTER 6

17. What is the meaning of the term "heart"?
18. What was the "balm in Gilead"?
19. Will all prophecies be fulfilled literally?

ACKNOWLEDGMENTS

APPRECIATION is expressed to the following publishers and authors for permission to use copyrighted selections:

Westminster Press, Philadelphia, to use quotations from *The Cross in the Old Testament,* by H. Wheeler Robinson, and *A History of Israel,* by John Bright.

Oxford University Press, London, to use a quotation from *Jeremiah, His Time and His Work,* by Adam C. Welch.

The Macmillan Company, New York, to use a quotation from *The Modern Use of the Bible,* by Harry Emerson Fosdick.

Abingdon Press, New York and Nashville, to quote from *Jeremiah,* by Elmer A. Leslie, and *Jeremiah: Prophet of Courage and Hope,* by J. Philip Hyatt.

Harper & Brothers, New York, to quote from *The Rebel Prophet,* by T. Crouther Gordon.

C. Frederic Jefferson, administrator of the estate of Charles E. Jefferson, for permission to use a quotation from *Cardinal Ideas of Jeremiah,* by Charles E. Jefferson.

John Knox Press, Richmond, to quote from *The Layman's Bible Commentary.*

W. F. Henderson, Edinburgh, to quote from *Jeremiah,* by Alexander Stewart.

Fleming H. Revell Company, Westwood, New Jersey, to quote from *Studies in the Prophecy of Jeremiah,* by G. Campbell Morgan.